I met Fern and her unforgettable mouse friend Sniffy more than ten years ago. Back then, I didn't fully grasp the boundless depths of Fern's creativity. Over the years, my admiration for her work has grown exponentially as I learned that to know her is to be dazzled by her. Pick up this book if you want to be inspired. Pick up this book if you want to be reminded of the power of storytelling to preserve traditions and nurture relationships. Pick up this book if you want to be reconnected to the feelings of awe and wonder that may have faded when you left childhood. Whatever the reason, add this book to your collection today. You'll be glad you did!

–Tracy Swinton Bailey, PhD.
Non-profit leader, activist, author

Fern's book, *Epic Grandparenting*, is epic indeed! To read it was an adventure as I wondered what creative activity this resourceful grandmother would think of next–an activity to learn from, to challenge creative muscles, or to just relax and enjoy during a week spent with cousins at "Oma's Camp." Learn a new language, anyone? A crazy song? Bake cinnamon buns? Play with Sniffy, Nibbles, and Twitch? This gentle, loving book packed with projects, photos, and stories emphasized for me the influential role grandparents play in the lives of their grandchildren.

–Angelina Fast-Vlaar
Retired college instructor, award-winning author
www.angelinafast.com

Going to Gramma's house has never been so much fun! Fern's creative and diverse ideas for games, activities, and learning experiences make this book an excellent resource, not only for grandparents but for parents, teachers, and anyone seeking the pleasure of enriching the lives of young children. I love, love, loved it!

–Linda Toffolo
Mother, grandmother, retired elementary school teacher

Fern Boldt has written an inspirational, creative, and funny book. Her highly relational style is novel and lots of fun. Her approach to active grandparenting is something I want to try with my own grandchildren.

–Linda Lensink
Writer, retired teacher, grandmother of four

Epic
GRANDPARENTING

Dozens of Creative Ideas for Entertaining Children

FERN BOLDT

Fern Boldt

ISBN: 978-1-4866-2088-3
eBook ISBN: 978-1-4866-2089-0

Printed in Canada

Word Alive Press
119 De Baets Street Winnipeg, MB R2J 3R9
www.wordalivepress.ca

Cataloguing in Publication information can be obtained from Library and Archives Canada.

I dedicate this book to my grandchildren
(Caitlin, Amanda, Nicholas, Melanie, Vincent, Alyssa, Ashley, Owen, and Rylie)
and to my great-grandchildren
(Arielle, Adrian, and Elijah).
Elijah is the only one who didn't come to Oma's Camp,
as he was born the year the camps ended.

Contents

Acknowledgements

Books don't write themselves. They need help from countless people. Besides the author, who laboured over the script for five years, here are some special people who helped bring this book to you:

My friends, who read the script and encouraged me to publish it.

My critique partner, Dianne Matich, whose expertise in writing polished this story to make it shine.

Dianne's grandson, Charlie Webb, for suggesting the title, *Epic Grandparenting*. You're destined for greatness, Charlie!

My editor, Evan Braun, whose skills I have come to appreciate through several other projects.

Word Alive Press, who carefully set up the book and readied it for publication. This is my third book with them.

My dear husband Peter, who puts up with my long hours pecking on the computer.

My sons and daughters-in-law, who entrusted their children into my care for days at a time.

My daughter-in-law Catherine for getting Oma's Camp started in 2003 by taking five grandkids and me to Myrtle Beach for a week of fun by the ocean.

My daughter-in-law Michelle for accompanying us on our trip to Ottawa by train with four of the children.

And, most importantly, this book is only possible because I have nine of the greatest grandkids in the world, plus three more from the next generation. You are my joy, my fun, and my life!

Foreword

I met Fern Boldt in May 2011 at a Society of Children's Book Writers and Illustrators event in Niagara Falls, Ontario. We found ourselves in the same workshop group and instantly connected. Her workshop piece was a humorous picture book about three mice, Sniffy and Nibbles and Twitch. She wrote this story originally for her grandchildren, but she wanted to expand the story's audience. I could imagine how much joy those stories must have brought to her grandchildren's young faces, but also how much happiness it had brought to Fern to write for them.

Over the last nine years, Fern and I have cemented a friendship based on so many of the things we have in common: our interest in children's books, our proximity in age, and our love for grandchildren. I was new to being a grandparent, and Fern was the experienced grandma. She shared her stories of Oma's Camp, the activities she and her grandkids did, and how much fun they had. We inspired each other in different ways, encouraging each other through the various writing projects we completed. Fern put out one book after another. But the one she needed to write was this one.

As my grandchildren grew, I looked to Fern to help with my summer bubby camps. On a weekend getaway with a group of writers, Fern taught us all the game of Dutch Blitz. What a hoot we had. It wasn't long before I taught the game to my own grandchildren. It's become one of their favourite games to play with me and each other. She renewed my knowledge of the children's songs and verses. She was a great reminder to me that being a grandma is as much fun for us as it is for the grandchildren. That is why this book is so important.

Epic Grandparenting is the perfect name for Fern's book. She is an epic grandmother and great-grandmother. She's always imagining new ways to spend precious time with her little ones and not-so-little teens, and even grown adults. This book is full of unique ideas from games and songs to recipes and even projects big and small. If you're going to become a grandparent, or if you are one already, this book is for you.

American writer and author Alex Haley has said, "Nobody can do for little children what grandparents do. Grandparents sort of sprinkle stardust over the lives of little children."[1] *Epic Parenting* by Fern Boldt helps grandparents do just that: sprinkle stardust over the lives of our grandchildren.

–Dianne Matich M.F.A.
Children's writer and editor

---

1 "Alex Haley Quotes," *BrainyQuote*. Date of access: October 27, 2020 (https://www.brainyquote.com/authors/alex-haley-quotes).

Introduction

Help! I'm a grandmother! Now what? Do you want to have fun with your grandchildren, but you don't know what to do with these rambunctious little people? Never fear. *Epic Grandparenting* is here!

But grandparenting is not for wimps. If you haven't kept the grandkids for a full week or more, you have no idea how many knots you'll need to tie in the end of your rope by the time they go home.

What if they're not used to eating your food? Do you find something they will eat, or let them go hungry?

If they don't want to put on their pyjamas or brush their teeth before bedtime, what would you resort to? "Okay," you may tell them. "Sleep in your clothes and let your teeth rot!"

If they want to go to the beach, how much stuff can they take along? Worse yet, how much will you allow them to bring back? (Not counting all that sand on their feet.)

If you only have bunkbeds, who gets to sleep on the top? Ever heard of taking turns, kids?

If they can't fall asleep right away, how long will you let them read or play on their iPads? They're too old to hold and rock to sleep.

If they don't want a bath and wash their hair, how many days should you allow them to go before cleaning up?

I've had so much fun with my nine grandchildren and three great-grandchildren. Several are now in their twenties, but they still love to come to our house to chat. Our close relationships fostered at Oma's Camp continue. They keep surprising me and bringing great joy.

One Brick at a Time

Did you ever have one paragraph of a book jump out at you, giving you immediate direction for the path ahead? That's what happened to me as I read Dinty W. Moore's book, *Crafting the Personal Essay: A Guide for Writing and Publishing Creative Nonfiction.*

In it, he says that writing a book is like building a clay brick wall. Each story in the book represents one brick. He imagines digging clay out of the ground, forming bricks from it, and then baking those bricks. He suggests making each one as well as possible and then stacking them off to the side. Soon he has several piles of bricks, but he doesn't know for sure what his wall is going look like in the end.[2]

Spurred by that image, I began making "bricks" for my new book, *Creative Grandparenting*. The first brick will show how I made pyjamas for all eight of the grandchildren and myself out of

---

2 Dinty W. Moore, *Crafting the Personal Essay: A Guide for Writing and Publishing Creative Nonfiction* (Cincinnati, OH: Writer's Digest Books, 2010).

happy face material. I designed a funny instruction booklet to accompany each set. Another brick might be about taking the grandchildren to the ocean. Yet another may tell of how I taught them Spanish during one of my Oma's Camp sleepovers.

I'll talk about Oma's Sewing Camp, where five grandchildren between the ages of six and fourteen sewed their own pyjama bottoms. At Oma's Writing and Illustrator Camp, I taught them how to write stories and then edited them. I invited a real illustrator to teach them for a day. Those sleepover stories will all go into one pile.

There will be a pile of bricks with lists of games we play, music we listen to, and fun activities we engage in, like writing in secret code, going on scavenger hunts, and making candy necklaces.

Another pile will contain the mouse stories I've written for my grandchildren over the past ten years. Three stuffed toy mice—Sniffy, Nibbles, and Twitch—sit on Oma's shelf. When she's not looking, they come to life and go on wild adventures together—rafting, fishing, and surfing on the ocean. They go trick-or-treating, have a birthday party, and generally cause havoc in their little world. I imagine other grandparents will want to read these stories to their own grandchildren.

Brickmaking is hard work. It's messy, exhausting, and discouraging some days. But I envision what a sturdy wall it will become when I've placed all my bricks in position. My critique group will help me improve each story. I'll let friends read them and see how they respond. Then I'll rewrite and revise and rewrite some more. My goal is to make each brick as perfect as possible before assembling the wall.

I'll need help putting my final wall together—an editor, a cover designer, and a publisher. I hope it will one day be an inspiration to many grandparents and the special little people who have brought so much joy to their lives.

One
An Invitation to Oma's Camp

A week before Oma's Camp began, I sent each grandchild an invitation:

Hey, Kids! You are invited to Oma's Camp!
Dates: July 2–6 (Sunday to Thursday)
Place: Oma's house

POSSIBLE ACTIVITIES:
Swimming
Learning Spanish
Sewing
Baking
Hiking
Picnic at Queenston Heights
Going to a movie
Journaling
Scrapbooking
Writing
Artwork

Opa is going to make lots of tasty food for you. Together we can make cinnamon buns, cookies, or other goodies.

POSSIBLE PLACES TO VISIT:
Happy Rolph's Animal Farm
Port Dalhousie Carousel
The playground at Pearson Park
Have a picnic at Burgoyne Woods
Go mini-golfing

RULES:
No fighting
No whining or complaining
Eat whatever is served
Do whatever Oma says—or you might get water dumped out of your Patience Jar! (See Chapter Seven)

What happens at Oma's house stays at Oma's house!

WHAT TO BRING:
PJs
Sleeping bag/pillow
Clothes for five days
Swimsuit/towel
Jacket/sweatshirt/boots
Notebook/computer/iPad
Toothbrush (We have toothpaste)
Hairbrush/comb
Your favourite book to read at storytime
Your favourite stuffy, so you don't get lonesome
Lot of smiles, giggles, and hugs
Spending money ($20 for popcorn at the theatre, etc.)

Two
Activities at Oma's Camp

It's quite a challenge to keep all those grandchildren busy and out of trouble for several days, so I plan for numerous activities. I buy all the items we'll need and make all the necessary preparations ahead of time. Once they land on your doorstep, there's no time to further prepare.

Here are twenty-five activities you can do with your grandchildren:

Bubbles

Kids love to blow bubbles. Keep a container of solution on hand, which you can buy at any dollar store. It's best to do this outside.

You can find many recipes for homemade bubbles online. You can find a couple of them on the *DIY Network*.[3]

Stained-Glass Window Colouring Pages

Colouring pages help kids of all ages to develop creativity, focus, motor skills, and colour recognition. Give the grandchildren a page to colour, then turn on some great music and join them in the fun.[4]

Time for Ice Cream

One of life's greatest pleasures is taking the grandchildren to the ice cream store. After a long day of activities, my grandchildren told me it was worth the thirty-minute walk to get this treat.

---

3 Mick Telkamp, "The Two Best Homemade Soap Bubble Recipes," *DIY Network*. Date of access: October 20, 2020 (https://www.diynetwork.com/how-to/make-and-decorate/crafts/the-two-best-homemade-soap-bubble-recipes).
4 You can download and print stained-glass window colouring pages online for free or tear pages out of a colouring book. Here's a good place to find colouring pages on the internet: "Stained Class Window Coloring Pages," *Coloring Home*. Date of access: October 20, 2020 (https://coloringhome.com/stained-glass-window-coloring-pages).

ABC Scavenger Hunt

Find one object that starts with each letter of the alphabet. Print out a list like this beforehand. Whoever finishes their list first wins a prize.

A _____	N _____
B _____	O _____
C _____	P _____
D _____	Q _____
E _____	R _____
F _____	S _____
G _____	T _____
H _____	U _____
I _____	V _____
J _____	W _____
K _____	X _____
L _____	Y _____
M _____	Z _____

Sparklers

Kids love to play with sparklers. Make sure a responsible adult is close by to supervise lighting them and disposing of them when they're finished. It's a good idea to have a bucket of water on hand to douse them.

Go to a Movie

I love kids movies and prefer them to most adult ones. My favourite character of all is Donkey from *Shrek* and its sequels. "I hope you heard that. She called me a noble steed!"[5] I blurt out

---

5 *Shrek*, directed by Andrew Adamson and Vicky Jenson (Los Angeles, CA: Dreamworks, 2001).

this quote every time we drove through Steeds, North Carolina on our way to Myrtle Beach. My husband Peter always hoped I'd be sleeping when we passed that spot.

Check your local listings for movies you want to see with your grandchildren. I always pay for the price of the ticket, but if they want popcorn or other treats, they must bring their own money. (Hey, I have my limits.)

You can always watch a movie or video at home, too.

ECO Crafts

ECO craft materials are sourced specifically from the most earth-friendly suppliers with a focus on safety, sustainability, and renewability. They are alternatives to popular art and craft supplies.

Check the internet or your local craft store for ideas. Here are some examples that our grandkids made.

ECO crafts made by the grandchildren.

Face-Painting

Kids love to have their faces painted. If they're quite young, you'll have to do this yourself. If they're older, they can paint each other's faces.

Here's a recipe for homemade face paint. If you only need enough for a few kids, you may want to cut down the amount of ingredients.

INGREDIENTS

- 1 cup water
- 1 cup corn starch
- 1 cup flour
- food colouring
- 1 cup lotion
- 1/4 teaspoon vegetable oil
- spoon
- bowl
- container

DIRECTIONS

Add water, corn starch, flour, and lotion to a bowl.

Mix together ingredients and make sure the paint consistency is to your liking.

If you want to thicken, add more corn starch. To thin out the mixture, add water.

Add food colouring.

Store in an airtight container.

Oma having fun with granddaughter Rylie.

Finger Puppets

At Oma's Junior Camp, with my youngest granddaughter Rylie and my great-grandchildren Arielle and Adrian, I sewed these stacking finger puppets ahead of time. The children decorated them. They all fit inside one another. The internet, especially Pinterest, can provide you with an abundance of patterns. Your grandkids will be delighted!

Finger puppets made by the grandchildren.

Hopscotch

This popular game requires sidewalk chalk and at least two people, but more people make for more fun.

So how do you plan? A hopscotch course typically looks like a series of numbered squares. The first player tosses a marker (such as a rock or coin) into the first square; it must land within the confines of the square without bouncing out or touching a line. The player then hops through the course, making sure to skip the square with the marker in it. Players hop in single squares with one foot (either foot is fine) and use two feet for the side by side squares, one in each square. Upon completion of the hop sequence, the player continues her turn, tossing the marker into square number two and repeating the pattern.

A loss of turn occurs when a player steps on a line, misses a square with her marker toss, or loses her balance. Players begin their next turn where they last left off.

Be careful not to step on any of the lines. The first player to finish one full course for each numbered square is the winner.

Heart Matchup

For this project, the children draw faces or designs on a heart-shaped piece of paper, then cut them in half. They kept one half and I hid the other half for them to find the matching one.

WHAT YOU NEED
- Wrapping paper or construction paper
- Scissors
- Coloured pencils or crayons, if the kids want to draw a face or design on them

ACTIVITY
- Cut hearts out of construction paper (1 to 3 per child).
- Draw a face or design on each one.
- Cut each heart in half. Make sure each differs slightly, either in colour or in shape.
- Hide one half of each heart around the living room or outdoors; give the other half to the children.
- Encourage them to hunt for their matching piece.
- The first one to find all their matches wins. If they like this, hide them again.

Magic Tricks

Encourage the grandkids to learn a few magic tricks to surprise their cousins. You can find lots of interesting magic tricks online to inspire your budding magician.[6]

1. Have your child hold a pencil by the eraser and shake it. At a certain speed, the whole pencil will appear to bend like rubber.
2. If you want to surprise your friends, hold a spoon up so that it's facing them. Then slowly slide your hand along the handle. It will look like the spoon is bending.
3. Learn how to make a coin disappear without the audience noticing.
4. Show your friends how hard you can squeeze an egg in your hands without breaking it.
5. Using nothing more than a pencil and your hand, you can make it appear as though the pencil is magnetic.
6. Learn how to make a coin appear out of thin air.
7. Show your friends how you can make it look like you're walking through a regular piece of paper.
8. Make your friends think you can push a cup right through a solid table.

---

6 Kate Ward, "13 Easy Magic Tricks for Kids," *Care.com.* January 18, 2019 (https://www.care.com/c/stories/4051/easy-magic-tricks-for-kids/).

9. Make a card look like it has lifted off your hand and into the air.
10. You can learn how to make a cool, peeled, hard-boiled egg look like it fits through a hole in the top of a glass bottle which is smaller than the egg.
11. Make a trick card with a pair of scissors and some glue.
12. Show your friends how to turn water into ice using a bottle of purified water, a freezer, and something cold to pour the water into, like an ice pack.

Musical Water Glass Scale

For this activity, you'll need eight identical water glasses, a plastic spoon, a pitcher of water, and a set of measuring cups.

Arrange the water glasses in a line and then fill them up with varying amounts of water. Try to make the increments of water equal. For example, start with one-eighth of a cup of water in the first glass, then fill each succeeding glass so that it has one-eighth of a cup of water more than the previous one.

When you're finished, tap each glass with the plastic spoon and enjoy the sounds the glasses make.

Nature Scavenger Hunt

Give the children a list of items to find outside. Here are some examples of items I have used, although if any of these aren't readily available you can come up with your own.

• A pear	• A three-leaf clover
• A maple key	• A pink stone
• A weed	• A pine needle
• A feather	• A shiny white stone
• A small pebble	• A dark stone
• A maple leaf	• A purple clover
• A piece of bark	• A dandelion
• A bug (dead or alive)	• A blade of grass
• An orange flower	

Celebrate with a Piñata

Adrian, Arielle, and Rylie.

One summer, I bought a piñata for my granddaughter Rylie and great-grandchildren Adrian and Arielle. It was shaped like a minion, from the movie *Despicable Me*.

Before we strung up the minion, I suggested they all give him a hug and apologize ahead of time for whacking him. They felt so badly for him that it was difficult to persuade them to hit him! Make sure the other children are a safe distance away, so no one gets hurt.

Opa took charge of raising or lowering the piñata as the children swung at it. They eventually needed to have an older cousin break it open. Then they all scrambled to pick up the candies that fell out.

Puzzles

Kids and adults alike love this activity. My husband and I set up a puzzle many months of the year for anyone to work on when they come over to our home. It provides a great opportunity to chat and joke while looking for the next piece.

Choose a puzzle that's appropriate for the age of the children. Check the internet or local store for a limitless array of them. Value Village and other secondhand stores have them, too.

Play Dough

My first memory of play dough, or clay, happened in Kindergarten at a one-room school in Nebraska. I made a clay snake and chased a Grade One student around the outside of the school to scare him. The teacher reprimanded me, as this boy had a heart condition and wasn't supposed to be running. My life of crime could have started early!

INGREDIENTS TO MAKE PLAY DOUGH:	DIRECTIONS:
1 cup water	Mix dry ingredients in a bowl
1 cup flour	Add water, oil, and food colouring
1/2 cup salt	Knead together
2 tsp. cream of tartar	Get ready for some fun!
1 tbsp. vegetable oil	
Food colouring	

Reading

I read to my own boys until they were twelve, fourteen, seventeen, and nineteen—books like *Tower of Geburah* and *The Sword Bearer* by John White, *The Best Christmas Pageant Ever* by Barbara Robinson, and the Bruno and Boots series by Gordon Korman. As youngsters, they grew up on Dr. Seuss's silly books. I practically had them memorized. To add some interest, I occasionally changed some of the words, but they protested. "Mom! That's not what it says!"

I loved reading to them *Are You My Mother?* By P.D. Eastman. When I asked the kids, "Did he have a mother?" the youngest would blurt out with great passion, "Yes, he did!"

By the time the grandchildren came along, I had a couple of shelves of children's books. Reading became part of the daily routine at Oma's Camp.

Here are a few of their favourites—and, yes, every one of these books has a mouse in it.

Oma's collection of mouse stories.

Writing in Secret Code

Tic-tac-toe cipher is a simple geometric substitution of letters for symbols, which are represented by where the letters are positioned in a grid. The example key below shows one way this can work.

I made laminated sheets with the symbols and had the grandchildren write messages with non-permanent pens. They were thrilled when I deciphered the messages correctly. Then they erased them and started over.

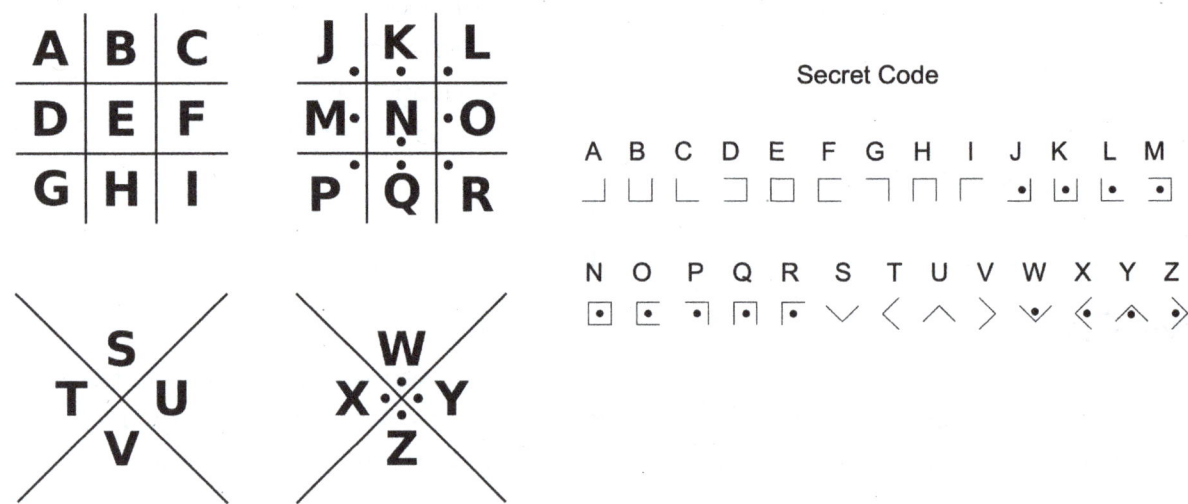

Skipping Rope

The grandchildren like to challenge each other to see how many times they can skip without making a mistake. It gets quite competitive. My husband Peter and I have sometimes joined in the fun, but we're not as good as the kids.

Get a good skipping rope, though, as the cheap ones don't work as well.

Swimming

When they were young, our four boys spent many hours in our backyard pool. When the grandchildren came over during the summer, they would race to see who could get to the pool first.

There are countless activities you can do in the pool. For example, racing laps, diving for objects, playing Marco Polo, seeing how long the kids can hold their breath underwater, and floating on pool toys.

Talent Show

Almost every Oma's Camp had a talent show. The kids picked a suggested topic and acted it out in front of the group. If my husband and I ran out of suggestions, the kids could make up their own. It can get quite creative, or rather hilarious. Here are some suggestions:

• Pretend like you're a favourite animal.	• Tell about your scariest experience.
• Tell the dumbest thing you ever did.	• What is one thing you never want to happen to you?
• What's the funniest thing your dad ever did?	• If you could change your name, what would it be?
• What's the nicest thing your mom ever did for you?	• Do a little dance.
• Pretend like you're eating worms.	• Make up a short story.
• Stick out your tongue and touch your nose. (One granddaughter could do this.)	• Do whatever you want for one minute.

Treasure Hunt

If you've bought a new toy or other surprise for the children, you can hide it ahead of time, along with clues to help lead them to where it's hidden. You start by giving them the first clue, which tells them where to find the next one. The more clues you make, the longer they get some exercise. (Sneaky Oma!)

Wii Fit

Wii Fit is a video game platform that uses a balance board for doing yoga, strength training, aerobics, and balance games. It's one of the greatest video game platforms ever invented! The children love to play on it when they come for a visit. At the end of each round, the machine calculates the players' score and shows the top ten performers. If they do better than the previous round, they can go up a notch or two. The kids think it's great when they knock their grandmother down the line or off the chart altogether.

Water Balloons

Kids and water balloons go together like peanut butter and jelly. This activity *must* be done outside, though, as it can get quite messy. And you never want to be the target of someone's mistakenly thrown shot.

Fill the balloons with water, tie the end shut, and have fun! We had a glass-top table that worked great for playing all sorts of water balloon games the kids made up. Once they wrote names on the balloons and had them crash into each other. Have lots of balloons on hand, so you can replace the ones that break.

They always wore silly grins on their faces before giving their Oma a soaking. I had a few in my arsenal, too!

Rylie and great-grandchildren Arielle and Adrian.

OMA'S CORNY JOKES

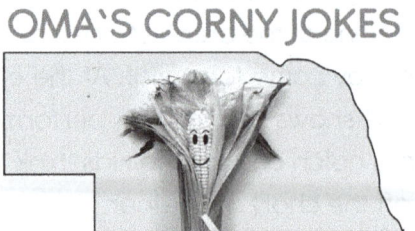

How can you tell a happy motorcyclist? He has bugs on his teeth.

Three
Games at Oma's Camp

When my granddaughter Rylie was five, I asked her to make a list of some activities she wanted to do at our upcoming Oma's Camp. You can see the list in the following photo. I hope you can figure them out! The first item says "draw pictures," then the next one "see who is taller." Her mother later noted that she should have added, "Pracktis spelling."

I incorporated many of her ideas into our next Oma's Camp.

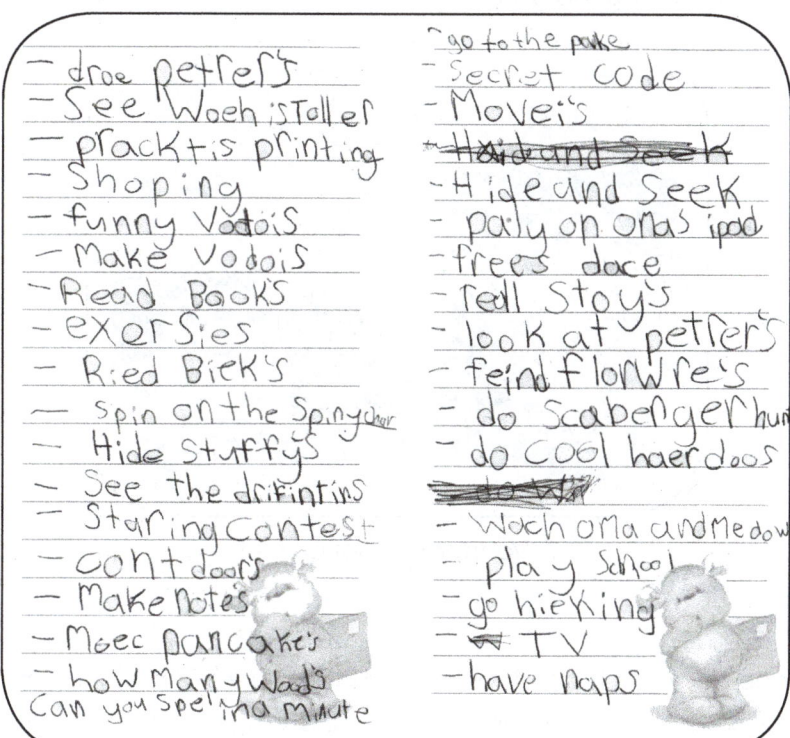

- droe petrers
- See Woeh isTaller
- prackt,is printing
- Shoping
- funny Vodois
- Make Vodois
- Read Books
- exersies
- Ried Biek's
- spin on the Spiny chair
- Hide stuffys
- See the drifintins
- Staring contest
- cont doors
- Make notes
- Moec pancakes
- how many wads
Can you spel in a minute

- go to the poke
- Secret code
- Moveis
- ~~Haid and Seek~~
- Hide and Seek
- paiy on omas ipod
- frees dace
- reil stoys
- look at petrers
- feind florwres
- do scabenger hun
- do cool haerdoos
- ~~do W~~
- Woch oma and me dow
- play School
- go hieking
- TV
- have naps

Granddaughter Rylie's list of suggestions for camp activities.

Board Games

I always told the kids, "If you're bored, play a board game."

Most families have a cupboard full of board games. Find out which ones the kids like to play and get in on the fun. The more time you spend with the children, the happier all of you will be. You can pick up all sorts of used games at Value Village or at garage sales.

Dutch Blitz

Dutch Blitz has been our favourite family game since 1980, when our four sons were young. Over the years, the grandkids and great-grandkids have joined in on the fun. It's a wild game! The mention of Dutch Blitz will send our family running for the deck of cards and a place to play it.

There's always a lot of hooting and hollering. If you're not quick, someone can whack your fingers in their haste to put down a card before you do. "I had that one! You beat me to it!"

When each round ends, there's a lot of moaning and groaning. But one of the younger grandchildren usually reminds us how to lose gracefully by saying, "Good game!"

I highly recommend buying this game.

A Vonderful Goot Game!

Freeze Tag

With this game, one person is It and tries to catch the others. When It touches you, you must freeze in that position until someone unfreezes you. Change who is It every few minutes until each child has had a turn.

Ghost in the Graveyard

The rules of this game are simple. One kid is the ghost, and the others lie in the "graveyard" and count to twenty while the ghost hides. Then everyone looks for the ghost. Whoever finds him first yells, "Ghost in the graveyard," and they all try to get back to their graves before the ghost catches them. The kids had *lots* of fun with this one.

Chase the Goose, or Grab the Sock

When I attended a one-room school in rural Nebraska, we had recess outside on the playground. In the winter, the older students made a giant circular path through the snow, with spokes crisscrossing it. If they wanted to be tricky, they would make a dead-end path, where someone could get stuck while being chased. Since the students ranged in age from five to about fourteen, it was easy for the older ones to catch us little ones.

I modified this game for my grandchildren and called it Grab the Sock. Each child tucked a sock in his or her back pocket or waistband. Whoever was It had no sock and had to get one by chasing someone who did. With sidewalk chalk, we would make a large circle on the driveway with spokes pathways across the middle, like a wheel. We chased each other around the circle, trying not to get our socks stolen. Whoever did lose their sock would become the next It.

Hide and Seek

Hide and Seek is a popular children's game which requires at least two players. One player is designated It, closes their eyes, and counts to a predetermined number while the other players hide. After counting, the player who's It calls "Ready or not, here I come!" and then attempts to locate all the hidden players. When It locates all players, the game ends. The player found first is the loser and is chosen to be It in the next round. The player found last is the winner.

Another common variation has It counting at "home base." The hiders can either remain hidden or can come out of hiding to race to home base. Once they touch it, they're "safe" and cannot be tagged. A hider must yell "free" when they touch base, or they can still be tagged out. But if the seeker tags another player before reaching home base, that person becomes It.

I don't think kids ever tire of this game. I played it with my four boys in the 1970s. They liked to shut off most of the lights in the house to make it easier to hide and scarier for the person looking for them, as they hollered "Boo!" when they were found.

This continued when the grandchildren started showing up—and more recently, the great-grandchildren, although this Oma is getting a bit out of shape for scrunching in a closet.

One time at Oma's Junior Camp in 2017, I hid under an old card table with a skirt around it. They looked everywhere and couldn't find me. When they were a bit further away, I meowed like a cat. They knew I was nearby but didn't suspect I was hiding under a table. We had a good laugh when they finally discovered where I was.

The Game of Jacks

I introduced this game to the children a few years ago. My great-grandson was enthralled with it and wanted to play it over and over.

The game requires at least two people, but it's more fun when you have more. You also need a small rubber ball and a set of ten jacks.

To decide who goes first, use the "flipping" method. Place the jacks in a cupped hand, flip them to the back of the hand, and then back to cupped hand. Some of the jacks will fall, and the player who ends up holding the most jacks gets to go first. That player then scatters the jacks into the playing area with a throw from one hand.

A game is divided into rounds of ascending numbers, which are based on the number of jacks each player must pick up per throw. In the first round, Onesies, the player throws the ball in the air and picks up one jack, then grabs the ball after it bounces one time. The player must pick up all jacks without missing the jack or letting the ball bounce more than once. If the player is successful, they move on to Twosies, meaning they have to pick up two jacks per throw), then Threesies, etc. If a player misses, then they lose their turn and the other player starts back from the beginning of Onesies.

The winning player is the one to reach the highest round, Tensies, picking up the largest number of jacks at once.

Grandma's Cookies

My grandchildren invented this game. When I found out what they were playing, I made them a batch of paper chocolate chip cookies to enhance their play.

One of them described the game like this: "I remember a game we cousins made up all by ourselves called the cookie game. We would start by walking up to 'Grandma's house' and knock on the imaginary door. The 'grandma' would answer and invite us in, then show us to our room and say, 'I love to make cookies, but you may not think about the cookies, you may not smell the cookies, and you may not touch the cookies. And the biggest rule of all is that you may not taste the cookies.' The object of the game is to run to the kitchen and take one cookie at a time back to your room without being tagged by Grandma. Every time we got a cookie, we would put a tally on our paper."

Red Light, Green Light

This game is especially fun with lots of children. Play where there's plenty of room, such as outside.

You should stand a good distance from the children and call out, "Green light!" The children should begin running toward you. Then say, "Red light." All the children must stop immediately, freezing in whatever position they are in. Repeat.

The first child who reaches you wins that round and takes the next turn calling out the light signals. You can specify skipping, hopping, or other variants instead of running.

Steal the Stones

This is an adaption of a game we played in our one-room school in Nebraska. Since we lived in corn country, we had lots of corn cobs to use, so we called this game Steal the Cobs. We played it at the side of the schoolhouse with kids of all ages from Kindergarten to Grade Eight.

We drew a line in the dirt and placed a pile of ten cobs about fifteen feet behind the line on both sides. Teams lined up on either side of the line and one or more would made a wild dash to "steal" a cob from the opposing team.

The trick was to steal the other team's cobs without getting caught and take it back to your own pile. If someone did catch you, you had to return the stolen cob to their pile and try again. The winning team was the one that took all the other team's cobs without losing all of their own.

For the grandchildren, we adapted this to Steal the Stones, as we had a lot of river rock around our house. It's a good way to work off some extra energy so the kids sleep better at night.

Simon Says

This game requires at least three people, but more would be better. Simon Says is a classic game that can be played anywhere. All you have to do is listen closely as the leader, Simon, gives you directions. If Simon says to do something, you'd better act fast. But if Simon doesn't start by saying "Simon says," and you do it anyway, you're out.

For example, if the leader says, "Simon says touch your nose," then the players must touch their nose. But if the leader simply says, "Jump," the players must not jump.

The object of the game is to follow directions and stay in the game as long as possible. The last player standing wins and becomes the next Simon. If you're Simon, the object is to try to dupe the players into following your commands when they shouldn't.

Snowman

This is akin to the old game of Hangman, but rather than expose younger children to images of violence, you can draw a snowman instead. Here's how you play.

1. Choose one person to be the "host."
2. The host chooses a secret word. The other players will try to guess the word letter by letter, so choose one you think will be difficult to guess, such as those with uncommon letters, like z, or j, and only a few vowels.
3. The host draws a blank line for each letter in the word. For example, if the person chooses the word *zipper*, they would draw six blanks, one for each letter. The host does *not* tell anyone else the secret word. For example, (_ _ _ _ _ _).
4. Once the word has been chosen and the players know how many letters it has, they begin guessing which letters are in the word by asking the host, "Is there an e in your word?" Generally, it's a good idea to start by guessing common letters, like vowels, s, t, and n.
5. If the players guess correctly, the host fills the letter in the blanks wherever it occurs. For example, if the word is *zipper* and the players guess e, then the host will fill in the fifth blank: (_ _ _ _ e _). If the players guess a letter that repeats, the host fills in both letters. If they guess p, the host would have to fill in both of those blanks: (_ _ p p e _).
6. Every time the players guess wrong, the host adds a body part to their drawing of a simple snowman. This is also a way to adjust the difficulty of the game—the more body parts you allow, the more wrong guesses the players get and the easier the game becomes.

The classic order goes like this.
• First wrong answer: Draw the snowman's head.
• Second wrong answer: Draw a larger circle for the middle of the snowman's body
• Third wrong answer: Draw an even larger circle for the bottom of the snowman's body.
• Fourth wrong answer: Draw one eye.
• Fifth wrong answer: Draw the other eye.
• Sixth wrong answer: Draw a carrot-shaped nose.
• Seventh, eighth, etc.: Draw one button at a time. For extra guesses, you could add a hat, scarf, sticks for arms, etc.

Once you draw all the available body parts, and the word has not been guessed, the players have lost the game.

Telephone

This game is ideally meant for children aged four and up. All the children sit in a circle or a line. One child whispers a sentence to someone beside them, then that person whispers the same sentence to a third person, etc., with everyone trying to repeat the sentence as close to word-for-word as possible. The last person to hear the sentence repeats it out loud so everyone can hear. Invariably some part of the sentence will have been lost in translation, and the resulting garbled message usually inspires a good laugh.

We played this one summer while sitting on the living room floor with a bunch of the grandchildren. The first person whispered, "Someone in the family has a ring tone." It became a bit distorted toward the end of the circle. When the last person revealed what they had heard, it sounded like, "Someone in the family has wrinkles."

Needless to say, we hooted at that one, because both Opa and Oma have a good deal of them! One sagging wrinkle after another, in fact!

Then the kids made up a little song with those words—"Someone in the family has wr-r-r-rinkles," and kept singing it for the rest of the week. Even years later, we still get a chuckle out of it when someone mentions it.

Wax Museum

For this game, you'll need to gather three or more players in a large room, which will be known as the Museum. The person who's It should then leave the room and count to twenty.

The players pose like statues, after which It comes back and pretends to be a museum guide. If the guide leaves the room, the players must choose a new pose. When the guide spots someone moving, that player becomes a tourist, and must follow the museum guide.

Anytime the guide looks away from you, at another "statue," you can quickly change your pose. Continue to play until only one statue is left. That player then becomes the new museum guide.

OMA'S CORNY JOKES

How can you tell if an elephant has been in your refrigerator?
There are footprints in the butter.

Four
Music at Oma's Camp

Turn up the music! The kids have arrived!

Music added an exciting dimension to our Oma's Camps. As I prepared for the children to come, I downloaded many children's songs from iTunes and put them into a special folder on my computer.

I cleared the junk out of our sixteen-by-thirty-two-foot storage room, outlined a running track on the floor with masking tape, and added several "safe spaces" in the corners. I set up a mini trampoline in the middle of the room, computer speakers for playing the music, and awaited the fun.

When the children needed some exercise, my husband and I turned up the volume and had them run around the track until the music stopped for a few seconds. Whoever didn't have a safe spot to stand had to drop out for one turn and jump on the trampoline. This continued until they became too tuckered out to run and happily returned to writing a story or some other activity.

We also played musical chairs by placing several chairs in the middle of the room, facing outward, and they had to try to grab a seat before everyone else when the music suddenly stopped. Even though one person had to be "out" every round, we always let everyone back in. No one wants to sit out the rest of the game, waiting for the others to be eliminated!

Sometimes the kids took turns controlling the music, so I could chase around with them. They thought it was hilarious when I had no place to sit.

Our young grandson Vincent found a great way to make sure he always had a chair... he carried it with him!

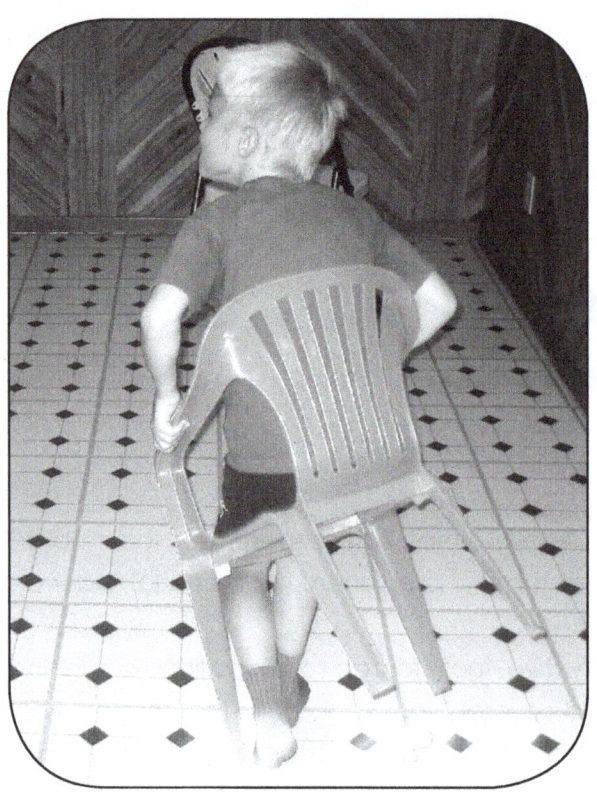

Vincent carries his chair with him.

Some years ago, I started to sing "You Are My Sunshine" to Melanie as I hugged her before she left for home. Not wanting Vincent to feel left out, I hugged him and sang, "You are my moonshine..." We dissolved into a fit of giggles when we realized how crazy that was!

Another time, Melanie caught me hugging her younger cousin Rylie and singing that song. She protested, "But I thought *I* was your only sunshine."

Apparently, *all* of Oma's grandchildren bring sunshine into our home.

I'm not sure if what I did influenced them to enjoy music as they grew up, but several of them have gone on to play the piano and other instruments. Ashley plays guitar and writes some of her own songs, which she performed at gigs with her music instructor in high school. She's now in the performing arts program at York University in Toronto. Owen plays the marching drums in his Air Cadet band, which has won several awards.

Siblings Melanie and Vincent have been singing all their lives. They often break into spontaneous duets while visiting our house. They know every song from Les Misérables by heart. Melanie also sang in a choir that had the privilege of performing concerts in several Scandinavian countries.

Vincent surprised me one Sunday by singing the American national anthem. But wait! Then he also sang the Canadian anthem, and then also anthems from numerous other countries. He can now sing more than fifty national anthems in their native languages. He once sang several verses of the Russian anthem to a visitor in our home from that country. She was duly impressed.

Five
Local Places to Visit

Occasionally we take the grandchildren to places of interest near where we live. Here are a few ideas for the Niagara region in Ontario.

Lakeside Park Carousel

Great-grandchildren Adrian and Arielle at the carousel.

For five cents per ride, you can experience the carousel's magic and its wonderful ability to bring out the child in you. It's a timeless tradition connecting our past, present, and future generations. The kids love it! Grandmothers, too!

The carousel features sixty-eight animals, including horses, lions, camels, goats, and giraffes, plus four chariots. Each animal has been hand-carved, and the horses still have real horsehair tails. The accompanying music is played by an antique Frati band organ which uses a system of paper music rolls to serenade riders.

Queenston Heights Park

Queenston Heights Park's facilities include two picnic pavilions, washrooms, a children's splash pad, tennis courts, a band shell, a snack bar, a playground, and seasonal fine dining at Queenston Heights Restaurant.

Have a quick picnic and let the kids loose to play!

Lester B. Pearson Park

This is a sizeable park in the middle of St. Catharines with two playgrounds, a splash pad, two soccer fields, two tennis courts, and a picnic pavilion. The grandchildren love to play here.

Vincent, Ashley, Owen, Rylie, and Melanie at Pearson Park.

Burgoyne Woods

Burgoyne Woods is a large park with lots of opportunities to explore, including passive open space, trails, a leash-free dog park, a playground, tennis courts, and picnic areas.

Super Putt Miniature Golf

This mini-golf course is a great place to take the children for an outing. We have many great memories of playing here, and the pricing is great!

African Lion Safari

We've been to the African Lion Safari with the grandchildren several times. Over one thousand exotic birds and animals roam free.

The silly monkeys climb all over your car or tour bus. Giraffes try to stick their head in your window. A couple of buffalo nearly butted our car once. Keeping the windows closed is good advice. Lions roar, snakes hiss, birds talk, elephants paint T-shirts... it's as fascinating for adults as for the children.

Happy Rolph's Animal Farm

This is the perfect setting for a family picnic. Our grandkids love to go here, pet the animals, feed the ducks, and play on the playground equipment.

Build-a-Bear at Myrtle Beach

Myrtle Beach is a tourist area in South Carolina where Peter and I had a winter home from 2003 until 2017. The city has endless activities for children. All the grandchildren visited us once or twice a year, so we have had a lot of fun together there.

The girls made this cute bunny for me. They each put a red heart inside of her and named her Elizabeth Marie, after their middle names. She happily sits on my bookshelf.

Ashley, Alyssa, and Oma at Build-a-Bear in Myrtle Beach, South Carolina.

Six
Things to Teach the Grandchildren

Basic Manners for Children

Children should be taught these manners at home, but if you notice that they haven't, or that they need a refresher course, these can be taught to them gently. There are lots of lists like this one on the internet.

1. Wait your turn to speak, and don't interrupt other people when they are speaking.
2. No name-calling. Even if it's in fun, it hurts.
3. Always greet someone when they come over to your house. Say hello so that they feel welcome.
4. Say "Please" and "Thank you" often. It shows respect and appreciation. If someone thanks you, respond with "You're welcome."
5. Clean up after yourself. Whether at home or at a friend's house, always pick up after yourself.
6. Practice good sportsmanship. After playing a game, no matter the outcome, be pleasant. If you win, don't gloat or show off, but be kind. If you lose, don't sulk or get mad, but be a good sport and tell the other child, "Good game."
7. Take compliments courteously. If someone praises you, be gracious and say, "Thank you."
8. Allow elders to go first and hold the door open for them. Don't let the door slam in the face of those behind you, but hold it until the next person can grab it. If someone holds the door for you, say, "Thank you."
9. When exiting or entering an elevator, allow those in the elevator to exit first before you enter. The same goes for buildings or rooms—if someone is exiting the building or room through the same door you are entering, let them exit first.
10. Respect differences. When people do things differently from your family because of diversity in culture, race, or religion, learn to respect that.

Table Manners

Whether in a restaurant or in a home, here are some basic table manners to teach kids.

1. Eat with a fork, unless the food is meant to be eaten with fingers. Only babies eat with fingers.
2. Sit up and don't hunch over your plate. Their wrists or forearms can rest on the table, or they can put their hands on their lap. You don't want to look like a Neanderthal.
3. Don't stuff your mouth full of food. It looks gross, and you could choke.
4. Chew with your mouth closed. No one wants to be grossed out seeing food being chewed up or hearing it being chomped on. This includes no talking with your mouth full.
5. Don't make any rude comments about any food being served. It will hurt someone's feelings.
6. Show appreciation by always saying "Thank you" when you are served something.
7. If the meal isn't buffet style, show consideration by waiting until everyone else has been served before starting to eat.
8. Eat slowly and don't gobble. Someone took a long time to prepare the food. "Slowly" means to wait about five seconds after swallowing before getting another forkful.
9. When eating rolls, tear off a piece before buttering. Eating a whole piece of bread looks tacky.
10. Don't reach over another person's plate to get something. Politely ask for the item to be passed to you.
11. Don't pick anything out of your teeth. It's gross. If it bothers you that badly, excuse yourself and go elsewhere to pick.
12. Always use a napkin to dab your mouth, which should be on your lap when not in use. Don't wipe your face or blow your nose with it, as both are gross. Excuse yourself from the table to do those things.
13. When eating at someone else's home or as a guest at a restaurant, always thank the host and tell them how much you have enjoyed it.

Learn to Set the Table

I taught the grandchildren how to set the table when they came over for Oma's Camp. When the table looks nice, the meal is more pleasant, since people enjoy food with their eyes as well as their tummies.

Teach your children and grandchildren to set a casual place setting, with forks on the left on top of the napkin, the plate in the middle, and the knife (blade in) and spoon on the right.

Once they have the idea, let them set the dinner table. Be sure to check their work and help them make any corrections before others come to the table.

Making Sounds with a Blade of Grass
As a country kid, I learned to make sounds by holding a blade of grass between my thumbs. Find a long, wide blade of grass and hold it tightly between your thumbs. Blow through the opening to make it vibrate.

Learn to Whistle with Your Hands
Whistling with my hands has been one of my favourite things to show the grandchildren. Cup your hands together and leave a small gap to blow a steady stream of air into them. If you do it right, you will hear a sound like a hooting owl.

How to Whistle with Your Fingers
I learned to whistle with my fingers from a cousin when I turned thirteen. I've used it many times to summon my boys for dinner, to get my family's attention, or even to settle a large group. They're usually a bit surprised to see an older grandmother letting out a shrill whistle like that. Anyone can do it with a bit of practice.

I wet the ends of my two middle fingers, tuck my lips over my teeth, push the bottom of my tongue back with my fingers and make sure the seal is airtight. Then give a soft blow until you hear a whistling sound. Keep trying until you succeed. But rest in between blows, so you don't hyperventilate.

Oma's Great Life Lessons, by Melanie Boldt
My Oma is a wonderful person. Every year she plans and prepares for half a dozen grandchildren to sleep over for three days to a week. She comes up with activities that suit children and teenagers of all ages and keep us all entertained. She's the world's best babysitter.

That's not even counting the countless weekend visits and sleepovers she's hosted. I'm sure that part of the reason family is so important to me is because I spent so much time at Oma and Opa's house with all my aunts, uncles, and cousins.

Needless to say, Oma has taught me many things over the years. Here are three that stand out:

1. Be creative. Be proud of what you make, no matter if you don't think it's any good. Many of the Oma's Camps I've attended have had artistic components, from puppet-making to sewing pyjamas, to drawing and writing. I've tried crafts that I never would have tried otherwise, and I'm glad I got the opportunity and the push I needed.

When Oma brought me to a writers' conference, I showed people one of the stories I'd been writing and received constructive criticism. I also learned how to improve my writing. Without Oma, I never would have attended that conference, which remains one of the highlights of my life.

2. The only person who can stop me is me. I can do anything if I set my mind to it. When I get writer's block, Oma gives me tips to overcome it. She helps all of us grandchildren with whatever crazy ideas we come up with (within reason, of course!) and encourages us to follow our dreams.

Her book, *Blemished Heart*, especially drove this lesson home. Oma overcame such strong opposition to achieving her dreams; what's stopping me from achieving my own?

3. Mice are cool! Oma loves mice, in case you hadn't noticed. She has stuffed mice, mouse calendars, mouse pictures, mouse books, mouse movies, and more. I can't say that's a bit much, since I had three pet mice in Grade Four. See, Oma? I followed your footsteps and got my own Sniffy, Nibbles, and Twitch!

OMA'S CORNY JOKES

Why do cats eat mice headfirst? They use the tail to floss.

Seven
Discipline at Oma's Camp

"I'm running out of patience with you!" What mother or grandmother hasn't said that a few times? Or many times?

I raised four sons, all born within seven years, so I know what can happen to the reserve of patience you start out with in the morning.

One day when I had said "I'm running out of patience with you" one too many times, I hit upon an idea: *Why don't I demonstrate to the boys how close I'm getting to losing my last bit of patience with them?*

I filled four jars with water and added a few drops of food colouring to each one. They each knew which colour was theirs. Whenever they did something that required discipline, I dumped a bit of water out; the severity of the "crime" determined how much. When the jar was empty, they received the promised consequence. Then I filled the jar again and gave them a clean start.

To be fair, I rewarded them for good behaviour, too. They could get more "patience" in their jar if they helped set the table, cleaned their room, or were kind to one of their brothers.

In theory, they could always have a full jar, but we're talking about little boys.

That worked so well that I decided to try it with the grandchildren when they came each summer for Oma's Camp. I explained how it worked and said, "When the jar is empty, I'll call your parents to come and pick you up." No one wanted to go home early, so they behaved themselves exceedingly well.

One year, they decided that their grandmother should also have a jar. I should have known better than to go along with that scheme! One day I said something they didn't think I should have, and they unceremoniously dumped some of my water out. That's painful!

Try this with your own children or grandchildren. It works wonderfully.

P.S. When my youngest son read this chapter, he said, "I used to purposely see how close I could get to the bottom of the jar." I can attest to the truth of that.

The patience jars, with different colours of water for each child.

OMA'S CORNY JOKES

As I suspected, someone has been adding soil to my garden. The plot thickens.

Eight
Food at Oma's Camp

The grandkids and I have always enjoyed cooking and baking together. It's a great opportunity to teach them new skills.

My husband Peter (Opa) served as chief cook during Oma's Camp as I supervised the children's activities. He made anything they asked for, within reason.

Their three favourite items for breakfast consisted of blueberry muffins, pancakes, and "eggs in a nest." We made the muffins from a mix, with a few extra blueberries thrown in for good measure.

Mouse Pancakes

Round pancakes are boring! So I showed the kids how to make mouse-shaped ones. Use one spoonful of mixture for the head, two for the body, a half spoonful for each ear, and a dribble for the tail. Like this:

When I made these for Rylie when she was little, I offered to help her cut them into sizeable pieces. As I did it, I hollered in a squeaky voice, "Don't cut off my ears! Don't cut off my tail!" I think it traumatized her a bit, because she said, "Oma, don't say those words anymore."

Oops! There goes some more water out of Oma's patience jar.

Great-granddaughter Arielle eating her mouse pancake.

INGREDIENTS

- 1 1/2 cups all-purpose flour
- 3 1/2 teaspoons baking powder
- 1 teaspoon salt
- 1 tablespoon white sugar
- 1 1/4 cups milk
- 1 egg
- 3 tablespoons butter, melted

DIRECTIONS

In a large bowl, sift together the flour, baking powder, salt, and sugar. Make a well in the centre and pour in the milk, egg, and melted butter. Mix until smooth.

Heat a lightly oiled griddle or frying pan over medium high heat. Pour or scoop the batter onto the griddle, using approximately 1/4 cup for each pancake. Brown on both sides and serve hot. (For mouse-shaped pancakes, follow the same directions.)

Egg in a Nest

INGREDIENTS

- Two slices of bread
- 1 tablespoon of butter
- 2 large eggs
- salt and pepper

DIRECTIONS

Cut or tear a two-inch hole out of the centre of each slice of bread.

Melt the butter in a large non-stick frying pan over medium heat until foaming. Add the bread slices. Crack an egg into each bread hole, season with salt and pepper, and cook until the bottoms are golden brown, about three to four minutes. Using a flat spatula, flip and cook until the second side is golden brown, about three minutes more. Serve immediately.

Mini Pizzas

The children have enjoyed making their own mini pizzas. You can buy ready-made dough, make your own, or use a can of refrigerated biscuit dough. Set out the ingredients and let the kids put on the toppings they like.

INGREDIENTS

- 1 can (16.3 oz) refrigerated original biscuits
- 1 cup pizza sauce
- 2 cups shredded mozzarella cheese (8 oz)
- 1 package (3.5 oz) sliced pepperoni

DIRECTIONS

Press each biscuit into six-inch round. Place on greased cookie sheets. Top each round with pizza sauce, cheese, and pepperoni.

Bake at 375°F for 10 to 15 minutes or until bottoms are deep golden brown and cheese is bubbly.

Cinnamon Buns

Another word for "love" is cinnamon buns. The grandkids can help pour the ingredients into the bread maker, roll out the dough, and spread butter, brown sugar, cinnamon, and some raisins on it before rolling it up. The children love the feel of the soft flour and squishy dough.

INGREDIENTS (ADD THEM IN THE FOLLOWING ORDER)

- 1 cup milk, warmed for one minute in the microwave oven
- 1 egg, beaten
- 2 tablespoons butter
- 2 tablespoons granulated sugar
- 1 teaspoon salt
- 3 1/2 cups all-purpose white flour
- 2 teaspoons yeast

FILLING

- Roll dough out to about a 12-inch by 14-inch rectangle and spread this on top:
- 2 tablespoons softened butter
- 3/4 cup packed brown sugar

- 3–4 teaspoons cinnamon
- Raisins, nuts, or chocolate chips (optional)

GLAZE

- 3/4–1 cup powdered sugar
- 1/2 teaspoon vanilla
- 2–3 teaspoons milk to make a creamy mixture

DIRECTIONS

Put slightly warmed milk, butter, beaten egg, sugar, and salt in the bread maker first. Then add the flour. Put the yeast in last. On the bread maker, use the "dough" setting.

When the dough is done kneading, put it onto a lightly floured surface. Knead in enough flour to make it easy to handle. If it's too elastic, cover and leave ten minutes.

Coat the rolling pin with a bit of flour to prevent it from sticking, then roll out the dough into a rectangular shape, about 12 inches by 14 inches and 1/4-inch thick. Then spread the filling over the entire surface of the dough.

Roll up the dough and pinch the seam shut. Cut one-inch thick circles with a sharp knife.

Place buns in a greased 9-inch by 13-inch pan. Cover with a tea towel and leave in a warm place for approximately 30 to 40 minutes, or until the buns have doubled in size.

Bake in the oven at 375° for about 14 to 15 minutes, or until light brown on top. When done, make glaze and swirl over buns.

Granddaughter Rylie icing the cinnamon buns.

Rice Krispy Treats with M&Ms

Who doesn't like Rice Krispy treats? This recipe is more interesting than most, as the mixture is pressed into a dixie cup with a popsicle stick in the middle of it. Those grandkids are going to love you!

INGREDIENTS

- 1/4 cup margarine or butter
- 1 (10 ounce) package miniature marshmallows
- 6 cups of Rice Krispies cereal
- 1 cup M&Ms candy
- 12 5 oz. paper cups (wax-lined works best)
- 12 popsicle sticks

DIRECTIONS

Combine the cereal and M&Ms, then set the mixture aside.

In a large saucepan over medium heat, melt the margarine and marshmallows together, stirring constantly. Combine the marshmallow mixture with cereal mixture and stir well. Mix completely until all the cereal is coated.

Spoon the mixture into paper cups and press lightly to fill them. Insert popsicle sticks into the centre of the mixture and press again lightly with fingers and cool.

Alternately, if you like, press half of the mixture into a nine-by-nine square baking pan and cool. Cut into squares.

Serve to a bunch of happy grandkids!

Teddy-Go-Round Cookies

Food is always more interesting with a bit of decoration. The grandkids had fun making these cookies by pressing the Teddy Grahams into the soft dough. Yummy!

INGREDIENTS AND UTENSILS

- 1 roll of slice-and-bake sugar cookies
- Teddy Grahams cookies
- Knife
- Cookie sheet and parchment paper (optional)

DIRECTIONS

Slice the sugar cookies and lay them on the cookie sheet, spaced a couple of inches apart. Press the Teddy Grahams around the outside edge of the sugar cookies. Bake the cookies according to the directions on the sugar cookie package. Then let them cool and enjoy!

Well, you can eat them before they cool!

The Ingredient Tower

One day the grandkids and I decided to make some treats at Oma's Camp. We gathered all the ingredients and started whipping them together. While I was creaming the shortening and sugar with the mixer, the kids silently made the rest of the ingredients into a tower behind me.

When I turned around, this is what I saw. Oma screeched! They laughed.

Vincent, Rylie, Owen, and Ashley made this ingredient tower.

Candy Necklaces

To make these candy necklaces, all you need is string liquorice and candy with a hole in the centre for threading. Mind you, it doesn't remain a necklace for long, because they eat them!

A Picnic in the Park

Alyssa, Melanie, Vincent, Ashley, Nick, Amanda, and Opa at Queenston Heights.

Each year we went to the park for one of our meals. This photo shows six grandkids with Opa at Queenston Heights, a lovely place near Niagara Falls, with equipment for the children to enjoy.

Set the ingredients in the middle of the table and let them make their own sandwiches. Easy-peasy. Then they're off to play. Happy kids, happy grandparents!

Dining Out

In 2018, we decided to take all the available grandchildren out for a formal dinner. Ashley had a friend whose family owned a Korean restaurant, so we ate there. Some of the grandchildren displayed skill with chopsticks, but not Opa and Oma.

Rylie, Oma, Opa, Owen, Alyssa, Nick, Vincent, Melanie, and Ashley at a Korean restaurant in St. Catharines. (Two granddaughters from California are missing from the photo).

Nine
Handwriting Exercises

Handwriting Exercises for the Grandchildren

Do you remember how you learned to print and write in elementary school? I do. At the one-room school I attended in Nebraska, we had fewer than twenty students altogether from Kindergarten to Grade Eight, with one young teacher for the whole school.

District #11 at Howells, Nebraska in 1952. I'm fourth from the left, with a ribbon in my hair.

We worked on penmanship exercises in small workbooks while the teacher taught other groups of students. In the early 1950s, the teacher punished left-handed children. She would whack a ruler across the back of a student's hand to make them go back to using their right hand. It frightened us little ones.

I printed each letter meticulously. If I made a mistake, I erased it and redid it. As a result, I learned to make my writing look as neat as the lesson in the book.

In the later grades, we also learned cursive, which many schools no longer teach. That's what inspired me to teach the grandkids.

One afternoon, when four of the grandkids came for a visit, I gave them handwriting paper and practiced printing and writing with them. I also taught them how to write their own signatures. Days later, when Alyssa had to sign her Canadian passport, she knew how to do it. She was so happy!

You don't want to make this seem like homework, though. If you do the exercises with them, spend the time chatting about their lives, telling stories, and joking with them. Kids like doing things with their grandparents, no matter what you suggest.

You can find sheets like this next one online or at your stationery store. Print off a few copies and keep them around for when the kids have nothing else to do. Here are patterns for some of the exercises I did with them:

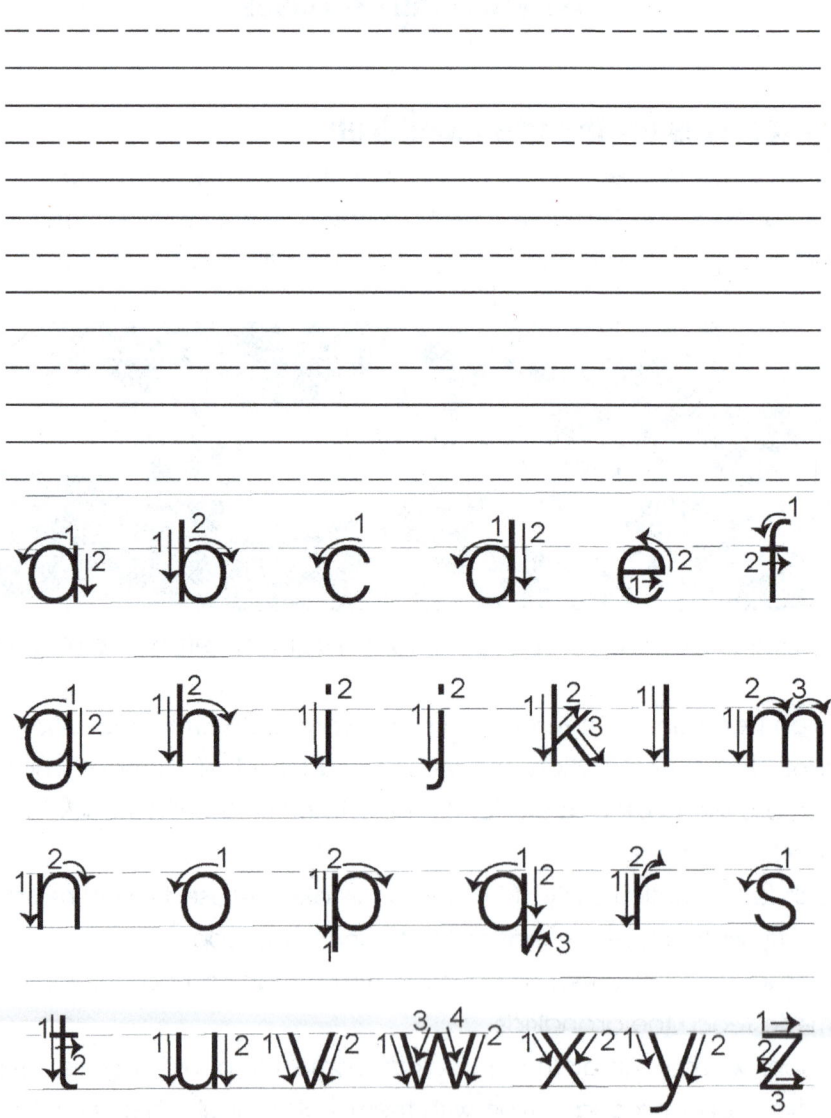

Granddaughter Rylie and great-granddaughter Arielle practicing printing.

Ten
Oma's Camp Reports

When each Oma's Camp ended, my husband and I wrote a report to the children's parents. Here are two of them:

Report on the Trip to Myrtle Beach

Our first Oma's Camp happened in 2003, when my daughter-in-law Catherine rented a van and helped me drive her three children and two of their cousins on a sixteen-hour trip to our second home in Myrtle Beach, South Carolina. It's astounding what one can learn from spending a week with the grandchildren. Here's what I learned:

1. Once they're "uncorked" at 4:00 a.m. to get an early start, there's no putting the stopper back in until 10:00 p.m.
2. It's wise to carry large Ziplock bags in the van in case someone gets carsick. (We needed three, all for different kids.)
3. Five movies make sixteen hours on the road fly by.
4. You can find license plates from thirty different states and two Canadian provinces on that long of a trip.
5. It's fun to bury Oma on the beach. (She wiggled her toes to make cracks in the sand and we had to keep repairing it.)
6. Sand sticks to your skin much better when you're wearing sunscreen lotion.
7. Hair washed in the ocean doesn't comb well.

Caitlin making sure Oma stays buried.

8. No matter how many hours you've been at the beach, it's always sad to leave.

9. With the amount of sand brought home every day, it's surprising there's any left by the ocean.

10. Mini-golfing with two six-year-olds doesn't remotely resemble real golf. It's more like a game of whack-a-mole.

11. Taking grandchildren shopping compares to taking a fox on a tour of a henhouse.

12. If you take a few artful bites out of a slice of bologna, you can create a smiley face and make Oma laugh.

13. Did you know that riding a scooter down the sidewalk is even fun for grandmothers?

14. Visiting an aquarium with live sharks, jellyfish, stingrays, and other sea animals is truly breathtaking. (Except for one camper who had an aversion to fish--and barfed.)

15. If someone can't go out for ice cream and wants you to bring back a cone for them, it's not a good idea on a hot day. One ended up with a cold splat in her lap.

16. You can plan a surprise birthday party for a seven-year-old with the help of four cousins without anyone snitching.

17. Playing the game of jacks with grandkids is seriously competitive and hilariously funny.

18. No matter how many books you read at bedtime, it's never enough.

19. A great bedtime game is "Ask Oma a Hundred Questions." How many brothers and sisters do you have? How did you meet Opa? What's it like to be old? What did you do on your honeymoon? (Yes, one did ask that!)

20. This can be reversed, and you can ask them about their own fears, hopes, and dreams. There's nothing quite like a listening grandmother.

A Visit to Oma's House

By the grandchildren: Amanda (thirteen), Nick (ten), Melanie (nine), Alyssa (nine), Ashley (six), and Vincent (six).

On Sunday, we arrived at Oma's house for what we thought was going to be four days of fun. Little did we know what was really going to happen.

We started playing freeze tag (True), but Ashley fell and hurt her arm. She had to have it in a sling the rest of the week (False).

We were playing with water balloons (T), but we accidentally soaked Oma, so she made us pop them all and throw them in the garbage (F).

We were having fun playing musical chairs, but Oma thought the music was too loud. We had to walk around so quietly that it wasn't any fun. We just all quit (F). (Oma had as much fun as the kids.)

We made our own pizzas (T), but they burned and tasted terrible (F).

We made cookies, which was the only comfort we had during the week. (T, but not the *only* comfort).

Melanie fell on the cement and scraped her knee. Ashley fell and got a bloody knee, too. Alyssa scratched Ashley in the pool. Alyssa burned her fingers on the stove when it was still hot from cooking eggs (T).

When we painted faces (T), Vincent accidentally spilled red paint on Oma's white shirt. That was the end of that! (F)

When we played Steal the Stones (T), Ashley dropped a stone on someone's toe. The piercing screams finished off that game (F).

Oma made us go on a scavenger hunt (T), but we couldn't find half the things on the list. She made us stay outside until we found everything (F).

Vincent kept getting nosebleeds. He bled all over his pillow. Oma put cool washcloths on him to stop it (F).

We weren't supposed to take food into the family room, but someone spilled his orange juice all over the carpet. Boy, was Oma angry! (T, but it was apple juice and wiped up without a fuss.)

We went on a treasure hunt. We ran upstairs, downstairs, outside, and all over the place. What a disappointment to find just one little cheap gift at the end of the hunt (T).

We were supposed to go swimming twice a day, but whenever someone started fighting, Oma made us get out of the water, even though the time wasn't up (F).

We were going to watch the movie *Garfield* in the theatre, but it was only on in the afternoon. We had to stay home and watch a boring video. (T, but the DVD was *Lord of the Rings*.)

Opa and Oma took us to the carousel (T), but there were so many kids in line that we only got one ride (F). The pop machine didn't work (T), so we had to go away thirsty (F).

Oma had stickers for us to put on our charts for being good. Well, we hardly ever got one (F).

We played Wax Museum in the basement in the dark. Ashley broke the flashlight. We had to stop the game so no one would step on the broken pieces (T).

We had a picnic at Queenston Heights (T). The sandwiches tasted awful. There was nothing to play on, so we went home (F).

We played Telephone. Someone started by saying, "Someone in the family has a ring tone." By the time it got around to the last person, she said, "Someone in the family has wrinkles!" Opa got a good laugh out of that one (T).

We each received three sparklers to light after dark one night. The wind kept blowing out the matches. When we finally did get them going, it was fun. We put the hot sparklers in a pail of water to cool them off (T).

That was the best thing of all the bad things. I don't know if we'll go back next year or not (F).

OMA'S CORNY JOKES

What lies at the bottom of the ocean and twitches? A nervous wreck.

Eleven
Oma's Spanish Camp

What language do you speak besides English? Have you ever tried to teach it to your grandchildren? Even a few words and phrases will help you bond with the next generation. My husband Peter speaks four languages. He may have sparked interest in our family to do the same.

Peter and I learned Spanish at a school on the Texas-Mexican border before travelling to Panama as missionaries in 1968. Spanish is such a beautiful language. I still communicate with one of my Panamanian students on Facebook.

In Canada, all students learn some French, as that is our country's second language. Two of our grandchildren, Melanie and Vincent, attended French-only schools from Kindergarten to Grade Twelve. Both are fully bilingual, as they also spoke it at home with their mother, who grew up in the province of Quebec.

Many years ago, I had a computer program called Mia's Language Adventure, the Kidnap Caper, which was useful for teaching Spanish to children. The grandchildren often played it when they came over for visits. They became fascinated with learning a new language and enthusiastically agreed to my suggestion of teaching them more at our next get-together. Thus, our annual week in 2006 and 2007 became Oma's Spanish Camp. Each grandchild chose a Hispanic name for the week. "I want to be Maria!" "Call me Carlos!"

I made flashcards with English on one side and Spanish on the other.

Common greetings in Spanish

· hola (hello) · buenos días (good morning) · buenas tardes (good afternoon) · buenas noches (good evening or good night)	· Adiós (goodbye) ·¿Cómo te llamas? (What is your name?) · Me llamo _____. (My name is _____.)	·¿Cuántos años tienes? (How old are you?) · Tengo diez años. (I am ten years old.) · Te quiero. (I love you.)

Colours in Spanish

Teaching the colours is easy, as you can spell the words using that colour of ink to print the words:

· azul (blue) · naranja (orange) · morado (purple)	· gris (grey) · rojo (red) · amarillo (yellow)	· marrón (brown) · negro (black) · rosa (pink)

Counting in Spanish

Kids love to count in another language. Here are the numbers from one to ten. If that goes well, you can go up to twenty.

1–uno
2–dos
3–tres
4–cuatro
5–cinco
6–seis
7–siete
8–ocho
9–nueve
10–diez

Days of the Week

• lunes (Monday)	• viernes (Friday)	• hoy es (today is)
• martes (Tuesday)	• sábado (Saturday)	• mañana es (tomorrow is)
• miércoles (Wednesday)	• domingo (Sunday)	• ayer fue (yesterday was)
• jueves (Thursday)		

The Family

Another idea is to learn the words to describe the members of your family. You can use illustrations from the internet or photos of your own family to show who each person is:

• el papá (the father)	• el bebé (the baby)	• la hermana (the sister)
• la mamá (the mother)	• la hija (the daughter)	• el hermano (the brother)
• el abuelo (the grandfather)	• el hijo (the son)	• la familia (the family)
• la abuela (the grandmother)		

Clothes in Spanish

• el sueter (the sweater)	• los zapatos (the shoes)	• los pantalones cortos (shorts)
• los pantalones (the pants)	• los calcetines (the socks)	• el abrigo (the jacket/coat)
• la camisa (the shirt)	• el vestido (the dress)	• la ropa (the clothes)
• el pijama (pyjamas)		

Body Parts in Spanish

• el cuerpo (the body)	• la boca (the mouth)	• la mano (the hand)
• la oreja (the ear)	• la cabeza (the head)	• la rodilla (the knee)
• el ojo (the eye)	• la cara (the face)	• el dedo (the finger)
• la nariz (the nose)	• el brazo (the arm)	• la pierna (the leg)
		• el pie (the foot)

I tested them later in the week with this little quiz:

1. The shirt is blue. La camisa es azul. _____

2. My name is _____, _____

3. I'm ____ years old. _____

4. Good morning. _____

5. I have one brother. _____

6. Today is Saturday. _____

7. The dress is purple. _____

8. Good afternoon. _____

9. Carlos is the baby. _____

10. The shoes are black. _____

11. Good night. _____

12: Yesterday was Friday. _____

13. The pyjamas are pink. _____

14. The sweater is green. _____

15. The jacket is red. _____

16. Goodbye. I love you! _____

The grandchildren have learned many languages over the years. Caitlin spent six months in Italy with a national family. She is also fluent in Spanish, speaks some French, and is studying Russian.

Nick, who speaks English and French, is studying Russian and German. He has a university degree in International Studies.

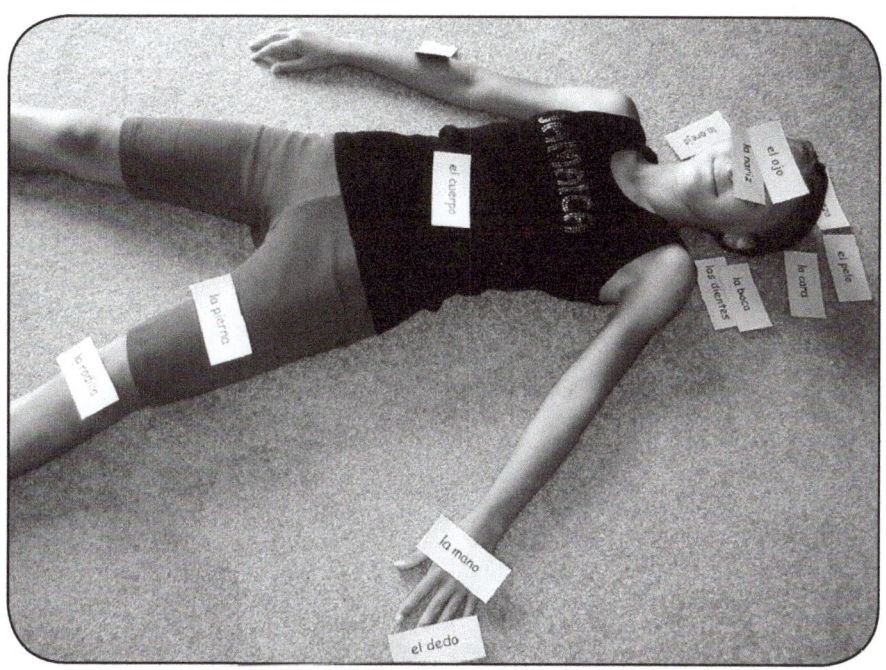

Melanie after her cousins had placed the cards on the proper parts of her body.

Melanie majored in French at university, and Vincent can sing the national anthem of more than fifty countries in their native languages. He used YouTube to teach himself how to pronounce the lyrics of each song properly.

The other grandchildren speak English and as much French as they learned in school.

Do as little or as much as you like to teach your grandchildren your native language. One day, when they're travelling abroad, they may be able to communicate with someone in the local language. You'll probably hear about it!

And it's quite the thrill to hear them say "I love you" in your own language. Ours learned to tell Opa in Plautdietsch (Low German), "Etj sie die goot." (Pronounced "Etch zee dee goat.") It never fails to bring a smile to his face.

OMA'S CORNY JOKES

Energizer bunny arrested. Charged with battery.

Twelve
Oma's Sewing Camp

When my youngest son Ted was little, he suddenly noticed a hole in his sock. He whipped it off and threw it onto his grandmother's lap to mend. When my husband and I laughed, he said, "Well, I didn't want her to sew up my foot!"

Later, he asked me, "When you're the grandmother, who's going to mend *my* children's socks?" That's when I realized that the skills had to be passed on from one generation to the next.[7]

Peter bought my first sewing machine in the early 1970s. I took lessons and learned to make clothes, hand puppets, and stuffed animals for my four sons, including a giant Bugs Bunny and Sylvester for the youngest two.

When the grandchildren arrived, nine of them over the next seventeen years, I sewed countless dresses, hand puppets, stuffed animals, small sleeping bags for their bears, oodles of doll clothes, bedding for a doll's poster bed, a life-sized stuffed boy for Owen, cloth purses for the girls, and a reversible Spiderman/Super O cape for my little hero Owen. I eagerly granted their wishes.

The grandchildren often sat beside me and watched each creation come into being. They wanted to learn how to sew, too, and that's what prompted Oma's Sewing Camp in July of 2010. That week, five grandchildren between the ages of six and fourteen showed up to learn a new skill.

I started by taking them all to a fabric store to pick out material to make pyjama bottoms. Back home, I washed all the pieces to preshrink them and to wash out the dye. I helped them pin the pattern onto the material, and they cut it out themselves.

I had two sewing machines, so the grandchildren took turns making their own PJs. I showed them how to make French seams, which is like sewing a normal seam twice, and the seam allowance ends up encased inside a fold so there aren't any raw edges to fray.

---

7 My solution for darning socks, after Peter's mother could no longer do it: fling it into the garbage can, saying, "Darn sock!"

For the younger ones, I held the material and they pushed the pedal to make the machine go. I hollered "Stop!" when they came too close to my fingers. We had some near misses with one camper. (I won't say which one, but it wasn't the youngest.)

I told them to snip off the little threads after sewing each seam, or it might tickle them in the

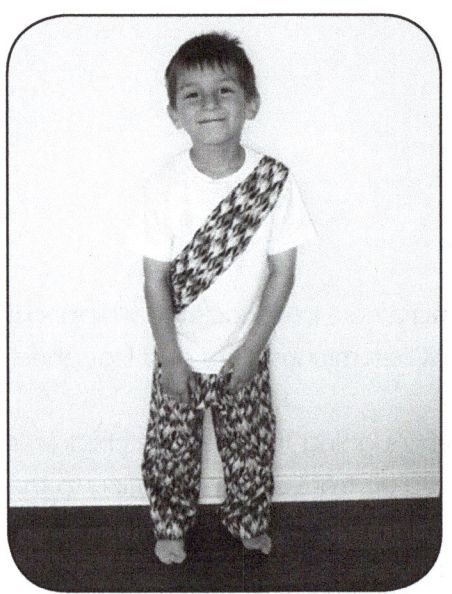

Six-year-old Owen.

night, making them think they had a spider in bed. We also tucked love into the PJs by kissing some of the seams. I told them the love never came out, no matter how many times the pyjamas were washed.

And that's what led to the idea of making everything we did "tucked with love."

The children decided to draw their own personal symbol to use at the end of their stories or drawings. When they finished their symbol, I duplicated it in a drawing program and made a fabric transfer to iron on to their plain white PJ shirt.

By the end of the week, five grandchildren had a new pair of PJs they had sewn by themselves. And here they are!

Alyssa (fourteen), Melanie (fourteen), Ashley (eleven), and Vincent (ten).

Did the sewing lessons bear fruit in any of their lives later? Well, yes! Ashley is now at York University in the performing arts program. Do you know what her favourite activity is? Designing and sewing costumes for their plays. And that's the joy of grandparenting!

Here is Ashley's response after reading this chapter:

> Hi Oma,
> This chapter made my day! J
> I'm so glad (or should I say "sew" glad J) that you taught me how to sew! Your creative projects have inspired me to do all the stuff I do in school today!
> P.S. I should remember to make sure that all my projects at school are "tucked with love."
>
> Love, Ashley

And here is Alyssa's:

> ☺ Those were the comfiest pyjama pants I've ever owned! Alyssa

Charlie, the Abducted Twin

When Owen turned four, I made up a little children's story for him about how someone had abducted his "twin" Charlie from the hospital when they were born. According to the story, Opa and I had discovered years later that a little boy who looked just like Owen had lived with a lady next door. He'd liked the same food and had the same allergies as Owen. Opa had called the authorities, who confirmed their suspicions and returned the little boy to his family. (Remember, this is fiction.)

I made Owen a toy doll for his birthday that looked quite a lot like him, with brown hair and eyes, and a cake wishing them both happy birthday. It was so lifelike that he was afraid of it for a long time.[8]

Charlie and Owen at their fourth birthday party

Opa's Memory Pillows for the Grandchildren

After Peter's diagnosis of Parkinson's in 2016, we made some adjustments to make life easier for him. We replaced his button-down shirts with golf shirts.

---

8 Once, when Owen needed a clean shirt for picture day at school, his dad borrowed Charlie's, because they wore the same size.

When I searched the internet for ideas to reuse his old shirts, I discovered a new concept—memory pillows. I then learned to make them for the grandchildren. I made a nineteen-inch square cardboard pattern for the front and back of the shirt, a six-by-nine-inch rectangle for the bow tie, and a two-by-three-inch strip to hold it together. I then had someone embroider this little poem:

This is a shirt I used to wear;
Whenever you hold it, know I am there.
Love, Opa

I took a photo of each one of these pillows with Opa and made pocket-sized cards to give to the children at Christmas. Each card had the photo on one side and a love note from him on the back.

The kids all love their grandfather and treasure both him and his memory pillow. They visit him as often as they can and give him safe hugs. Long after we are gone, they will still have a tangible memory of him in the form of these pillows.

A memory pillow for each of the grandchildren.

Opa and granddaughter Ashley. Isn't this priceless?

OMA'S CORNY JOKES

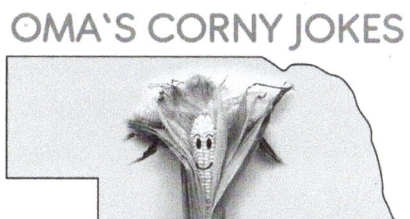

I'm reading a book about anti-gravity. I can't put it down.

Thirteen
Scrapbooks for Kids Turning Twelve

When our first granddaughter Caitlin turned twelve, I made a photo album of her life. A couple of years later, her sister Amanda received hers. Then life happened and their younger brother Nick didn't get his until much later. In the meantime, I learned how to create photo books online. I've been doing it that way ever since.

Here's the cover of Nick's:

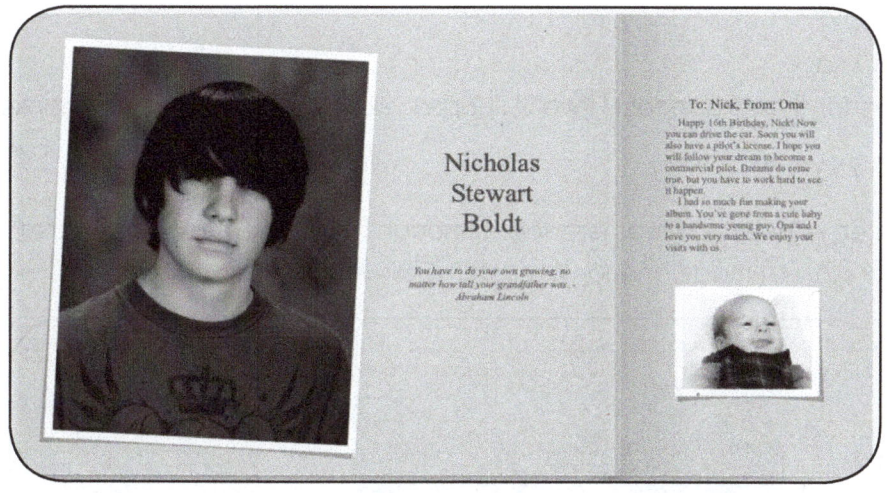

Thanks for the photo book. It was great looking at all the memories. We had a few laughs at some of the quotations, such as the Homer Simpson one. I appreciate the hard work you put in it.

—Nick

Cousin Melanie came next:

Dear Oma,

Thanks for the scrapbook! I love it! I hope I will be a NICE teenager! Thanks again!

Love Melanie

Months later, Alyssa received hers, too—although I no longer have a photo of it. Three years later, I made one for her sister Ashley:

And less than a year later, Vincent needed one:

I had a four-year break before Owen turned twelve:

I made the last one this year, as Rylie turned twelve in 2020. Her cousin Ashley designed the cover:

The last two have 111 pages each and around seven hundred photos. It takes three weeks to several months to design each one, but it's a treasure for them to show to their family and friends.

OMA'S CORNY JOKES

What has eight wheels and flies? A garbage truck.

Fourteen
Holiday Ideas

Thanksgiving

Getting together as a family at Thanksgiving is a great opportunity to express our thanks for one another and all the blessings we have received. In Canada, we celebrate on the second Monday in October, while our American friends mark the occasion on the fourth Thursday of November. Since I have dual citizenship, we often celebrate twice each year.

In our family, everyone who is available comes to our house for the traditional turkey dinner. There are usually a few guests, too. Each family brings part of the meal, so it's not a lot of work for any one person to prepare. I make the dining room festive with decorations, a beautiful table setting, and colourful place cards for each person.

For several years, I asked them to write or design something to show what they were thankful for. We put these items on the dining room wall for everyone to read and enjoy. Here are a few:

Nearly everyone made something.

Christmas

Birthdays! Christmas! Presents! Presents! Presents! When I first became a grandmother, I thought it would be so much fun to buy toys and clothes for the little ones. What I found out a few years later is that these kids not only had enough, but an excess of everything. I had to adjust my thinking and my giving.

Here are a few hints.

Ask their mother what they need or want. Otherwise you could buy totally inappropriate gifts. For my three great-grandchildren in California, some three thousand miles away, my daughter-in-law makes a list of gifts for the kids and a link to where we can buy them on the internet. I have them shipped directly to her house and she wraps them for Christmas. Easy-peasy.

After turning about ten, kids tend to most appreciate receiving money. They can go buy whatever they really want with it. I've also found that handmade gifts are more meaningful than purchased ones, like clothes for their dolls, sleeping bags for their teddy bears, or doll beds.

One time our eleven-year-old grandson Nick asked for a video game for his birthday. I made a duplicate copy of a Barney video cover—you know, the little purple dinosaur. I then encased his game box in the Barney cover and made it look like it had never been opened. I decided to spark it up a bit by wrapping it in five different sizes of boxes.

On the day of his birthday, he unwrapped and unwrapped and unwrapped! And when he saw the Barney cover, he was ticked. "That's not what I wanted. That's for little kids."

Upon opening it further, he discovered, much to his surprise, that it was indeed his requested game. It entertained the whole family for a few minutes. To this day, he still remembers and laughs about that.

A few years ago, I decided to try to be more creative than merely stuffing a few dollars in a card for them. I needed to take it up a notch.

In 2016, I taped a bunch of bills end to end, rolled them up, and put them in a cardboard tube (like the ones at the centre of paper towel or wrapping paper rolls.) I made a slit large enough to pull the bills through and wrapped it in Christmas paper. I attached a note to one end of the bills to wish each grandchild a Merry Christmas and then asked them to slowly pull on the tab. All of them opened theirs at the same time. They stood wide-eyed as the bills came out. The whole family enjoyed that.

I had to top that the next Christmas, so in 2017 I found an idea online about putting money in a container of play dough with the caption, "I thought you could use a little extra 'dough.'" I put the play dough in a plastic bag to keep it from touching the bills. I then inserted the money around the dough, closed it, and wrapped it for Christmas.

After the grandkids had opened them, they had fun creating all sorts of objects from the play dough. It gave them a fun activity to do with the cousins.

In 2018, I bought candy canes, a box with a giant chocolate first initial of each grandchild's name, a small empty box for hiding their money, and various other candies. I glued the candy canes to the largest box to make a sleigh, piled the rest on top, and tied it with a bow. It didn't take long for the kids to find the hidden treasure! And they could feast on the sweets the rest of the day.

In 2019, I tried a new trick on them. I bought small boxes at the dollar store along with lots of foil-wrapped chocolates. I hid some money in the bottom of the box, inserted a false bottom made from construction paper, and filled it with candy. They had funny looks on their faces when they opened the boxes, as they thought at first that the gift only contained chocolates. A few started to put their gifts away when one of the mothers suggested they dig a bit deeper. It was fun to see their surprised looks!

The candy box with the false bottom.

Fifteen
Travel Activities

The Alphabet Game (ages five and up)

One person chooses the right-hand side of the road and someone else the left. Each player looks for letters of the alphabet that appear on signs or license plates on their side. The object of the game is to point out all the letters of the alphabet in order, from A to Z. The first person to spot the entire alphabet wins.

Our boys often played this game while traveling, but we didn't let anyone know what letter we were currently looking for. Suddenly, someone hollered Z, and it was over. We also looked for the letters on both sides of the road.

Bury Your Horses

Have the kids be on the lookout for horses and cemeteries along the road. The first person to see a horse gets to claim it and add it to their count. The first person to see a cemetery shouts, "Bury your horses!" Everyone else but the shouter's horse count then goes back to zero. Repeat. The first one who counts to a certain number of horses wins.

Our boys counted all sorts of things while we travelled—transport trucks, red pickups, motorcycles, or whatever else they came up with. One time our youngest son Ted said, "I'm going to count chickens!" We all doubled over with laughter, because there are certainly no chickens running loose near a three-lane highway.

While driving in Nebraska, it was easier to count cattle. If we passed a farm with hundreds of them, you hit the jackpot.

Car Bingo

Cross out the items you see. The first person to get a full line vertically, horizontally, or diagonally wins a prize.

Horse	Moving truck	Deer	Red car	Convertible
Dump truck	Wild flowers	Jeep	Stop sign	Bridge
Blue car	Canadian flag	FREE!	Gas station	Yellow car
Dead tree	Bird	Sports car	Transport truck	Stalled car
Bus	Cemetery	Dog	Motorcycle	Cow

Connect the Dots

Game Play: Draw rows of dots, separated by a good half inch in a grid of 10 by10 columns. Each player takes a turn connecting one dot to another adjacent dot horizontally or vertically, one move at a time. After a while, the board begins to fill with a series of horizontal and vertical lines, some connected, some not. When a player draws a line that forms a square, that player fills the square with his first initial. The player who drew the closing line on the square gets another turn.

Objective: The game is played until all the dots become boxes. The player with the most boxes completed at the end becomes the winner.

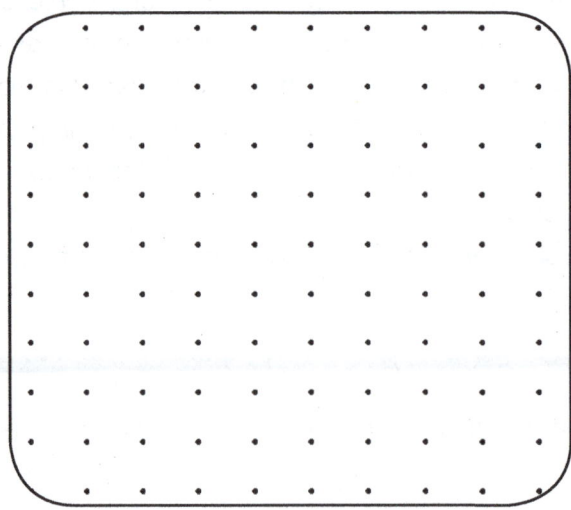

I Spy with My Little Eye

Two or more people can play this game. Player One spies something but keeps it a secret. The item should be something everyone can see. It's best not to choose something that will disappear, such as a motorcycle zooming past.

Player One says, "I spy with my little eye something that..." and ends with a clue, such as "is red" or "starts with the letter H."

The other players then take turns asking one question each. Is it inside the car? Is it round? Does it have wheels? Player One can only respond with yes or no.

If a player thinks he knows what the mystery item is, he can use his question to guess directly. Is it that barn? Is it that pickup truck? Is it Dad's sunglasses?

When someone guesses correctly, then he or she gets to choose the next item. This game can keep little kids happily occupied for a long time.

The License Plate Game (ages five and up)

Copy a map of Canada and/or the United States, then make a list of all the states and provinces to check off when you see another vehicle on the road with a license plate from that place. Try to find license plates from all fifty states and/or ten provinces. Whoever sees and calls out the license plate first gets a point. The person with the most points wins.

Storytime (ages eight and up)

Get creative by inventing a fairy tale. The first person starts with "Once upon a time..." and offers a complete sentence. Then the second person adds to the story with their own sentence. This continues with each person until the story reaches a conclusion.

You can either set a time limit, such as fifteen minutes, or make the goal to wrap up the story once every person has had the chance to say three sentences.

The Mile Marker Game

My husband and I did a lot of traveling with our four sons. It takes a great deal of ingenuity to keep so many kids from getting into trouble with each other for endless hours.

In the United States, highway markers are spaced at one-mile intervals. When driving sixty miles per hour, a sign appeared once every minute. We had the boys duck their heads down and count to approximately 60. The object of the game was to pop back up right at the next marker.

Our son Tom was especially good at it. One time when we were playing this game, a marker was missing. It was the only time he was "wrong." Anyway, it resulted in one whole minute of golden silence for us parents.

The game worked so well that I winked at Peter and whispered, "Let's try two miles." Two whole minutes of absolute silence! Ah! The luxury!

Road Trip Scavenger Hunt

With a scavenger hunt, the goal is to look for and find a predetermined number of objects. The winner is the person who either finds them all, or finds the most items on the list before time runs out.

Punch Bug

With this game, the first person to see a Volkswagen Beetle gets to punch someone else lightly in the arm and say, "Punch Bug blue!" (or whatever other colour the Beetle happens to be).

Tic-Tac-Toe

Make a three-by-three grid on laminated paper. Use non-permanent pens so that you can erase the marks after each round.

One person marks an X in one square of the grid, then the other players marks an O. Players take turns making their marks in empty squares, until one player manages to get three of their marks lined up in a row, whether vertical, horizontal, or diagonal. They're the winner! When all nine squares are full, the game is over.

Movies in the Car

We didn't have video players when our boys were young, but we sure made use of them while traveling with the grandchildren later in life. We made several trips between Ontario and Myrtle Beach with some of the grandchildren, and movies kept the children entertained for most of the sixteen-hour drive.

Sixteen
Oma's Writing and Illustrating Camp

In 2011, I sent an invitation to the grandchildren, inviting them to my newly conceived Oma's Scribbler's Squad Camp:

You are invited to Oma's Scribbler Squad Camp
Learn to Write and Illustrate
August 8–10, 2011
Attendees: Melanie, Vincent, Alyssa, and Ashley Boldt
Illustrator Instructor: Wendy Whittingham
Writing Instructor: Fern Boldt, a.k.a. "Oma"

Alyssa, Ashley, Oma, Vincent, and Melanie.

As the grandchildren grew older, I had to find something more challenging for them to do for a week. I invited Wendy Whittingham, a published illustrator from my critique group, to teach the children. The kids did some amazing drawings with Wendy's guidance.

Here are the results of one day of illustrating:

Vincent and art instructor Wendy Whittingham.

Alyssa with her drawing of Taylor Swift.

Melanie with her self-portrait.

Ashley drew herself as a baby.

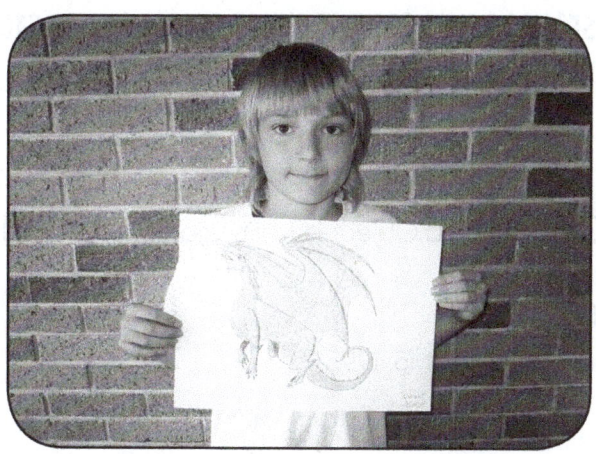

Vincent loves drawing dragons.

If you want to start with something easy, there are lots of examples on the internet. Search for step-by-step drawings.

For the other four days, we learned about writing. I bought a notebook for each camper and filled it with copies of the writing lessons: character sketches for the main character (the Big Cheese) and the less important characters (the Little Cheeses), story planning sheets, and identifying positive and negative character traits.

After they wrote a bit of their story, I edited it one-on-one with each child. This continued throughout the rest of the writing camp.

I showed them how to do a character sketch using my toy mouse Sniffy, who appears in many of my children's books.

Sniffy on his new skateboard.

WHO'S THE "BIG CHEESE" (MOST IMPORTANT CHARACTER) IN YOUR STORY?9

Character's Name: Sniffy

Male ☑ Female ☐

Human ☐   Animal ☐   Animated Object ☑   Dragon ☐   Fairy ☐   Other ☐_____

PHYSICAL DESCRIPTION

Age: 8 (his real birthday is August 15, 1995).

Height: 6"

Weight: 4 oz.

Hair: Fur with grey stripes.

Eyes: Black.

Skin colour: See hair above.

Favourite clothes: Au naturel!

Favourite colour: Blue.

Eating habits: Likes to nibble cheese.

Unusual features: He has large ears, a pink nose, is quite chubby from eating all that cheese.

Where does your character live? At Oma Boldt's house.

Mode of transport: Scampers or rides a skateboard.

What does his bedroom look like? He has one striped blanket and happy face pyjamas. Otherwise, a general mess.

Does your character have or want any pets? He doesn't want any cats!

SOCIAL DESCRIPTION

History and home life: Sniffy is an orphan. A cat ate his parents when he was one year old.

Parents: Chester and Pinky Cheeser.

Siblings: Two adopted siblings, Nibbles and Twitch.

Spouse: Too young to marry.

Children: Likewise.

Cultural background: Sniffy speaks English. He is non-religious.

Who are his friends? Nibbles, Twitch, Louie, the Cheeser family.

Who are his enemies? All cats, snakes, and large spiders.

---

9 I found the following character sketch sheet on the internet about ten years ago.

78

What are his prejudices: He's quite unbiased.

Favourite activities: Golfing, surfing, fishing, snowboarding, skateboarding, going to parties.

What are your character's three favourite places? Lake, ocean, mini-golf course.

Does he have any mannerisms (idiosyncrasies, quirks, oddities, foibles, peculiarities, habits, odd characteristics, tics)? He likes to count. He can't sit still for long.

What are your character's bad habits? Overeating.

What are your character's flaws? He's arrogant, doesn't listen to others.

INTELLECTUAL DESCRIPTION

IQ: High ☑ Average ☐ Low ☐

Education: He's in Grade Two in the local mouse school.

Highest grade completed: Grade Two.

Occupation: Student.

Hobbies or activities: Anything but schoolwork. He likes building things.

Favourite sayings: "Hokey Dinah!" and "Aw, come on, guys! What could happen?"

Favourite books, movies, music, or heroes: He likes to read mouse stories to Twitch.

Future plans: He doesn't think ahead! More adventures.

List three skills your character possesses: Fishing, rafting, golfing.

List three things your character dislikes: Cats, no cheese left in the fridge, Twitch screaming in his sleep.

List three of your character's favourite things: His fishing rod, his surfboard, and his skateboard.

EMOTIONAL DESCRIPTION

Personality: He's a lovable big brother to the other mice.

Strengths: Ambitious, courageous, decisive, enthusiastic, friendly, optimistic, self-confident.

Weaknesses: Thoughtless sometimes, arrogant, undisciplined, silly, disorganized.

Trauma in past: A cat ate his parents!

Ability to handle stress: "No problem!"

Good influences in past: Oma adopted him.

What is your character's goal? To go on another adventure.

What is his motivation? He has a restless spirit.

List three of your character's worst fears: Getting eaten by a cat, running out of cheese, running out of things to do.

Paradoxes (self-contradiction): He loves the ocean but is not a good swimmer.

Dreams: A cat-less society.

Sense of humour? Definitely.

Is he serious? Seldom.

Is he kind? Sort of, in a reckless kind of way.

Does he have strong feelings about anything? Because a cat ate his parents, he has a morbid fear of them.

Does he speak fast, slowly, or in an unusual way? He talks fast.

Does he listen to others? No, not usually.

What does your character need? He needs friends to have fun with.

What does your character want? He wants to squeeze every minute of fun out of every day.

Who is stopping your character from achieving those needs and wants? Lack of opportunity to get out of the house.

What is your main character's plan? To build a better cat trap.

How does the plan go wrong? He catches a skunk instead of a cat.

What does your character learn about him/herself? His best-laid plans can go wrong.

How has your main character changed by the end of the story? He's a bit humbler. He probably needs to go to obedience school.

Positive and Negative Character Traits

POSITIVE TRAITS	NEGATIVE TRAITS
Accepts authority, loyal	Rebellious
Affectionate	Distant, cold, aloof
Ambitious, motivated	Self-satisfied, unmotivated
Caring	Uncaring
Cheerful	Gloomy, sour, grumpy
Considerate, thoughtful	Inconsiderate, thoughtless
Cooperative	Uncooperative, combative

Courageous	Cowering, fearful
Decisive	Indecisive
Devoted	Uncommitted, hostile
Determined	Indecisive, unsure
Endures	Relents, gives up
Enthusiastic	Unenthusiastic, apathetic
Flexible	Inflexible, rigid, stubborn
Forgiving	Unforgiving
Focused	Unfocused, scattered
Friendly	Unfriendly, distant aloof
Frugal, thrifty	Wasteful, spendthrift
Grateful	Ungrateful, unappreciative
Hard-working	Lazy
Honest	Dishonest, deceiving, lying
Humble	Arrogant, conceited
Kind	Unkind, uncaring, cruel
Mature	Immature
Optimistic	Pessimistic
Positive	Negative

Reliable	Unreliable
Respectful	Rude
Self–confident	Lacks self–confidence

Other Lessons

During the week, one grandchild neglected to put a period at the end of each sentence, so I made this for her:

If you don't put a period at the end of a sentence, all the words will
L
  E
    A
      K

         O
           U
             T
So, put the "cork" in!
Love, Oma

I also helped them understand the difference between some other tricky words:
- You're = You are
- Your = It belongs to you
- They're = They are
- Their = It belongs to them
- There = A place
- We're = We are
- Were = Past tense of are
- Where = A place
- Then = A point in time
- Than = A method of comparison
- Two = The number 2

· To = A common preposition
· Too = Also or excessively

Owen, Oma, Ashley, Melanie, and Vincent writing a story.

Sometimes our grandchildren surprise us with their totally innocent honesty.

Granddaughter: "Oma, why do you colour your hair?"
Oma: "To make me look younger."
Granddaughter: "Well, it's not working."
Oma screeches: "It's not?"
Granddaughter: "No, your skin still looks old."

Oma wilts.
(Name withheld to protect the guilty, I mean, innocent.)

Seventeen
Stories by the Grandchildren

The grandchildren loved making up stories. Rylie, too young to write, dictated her creations to me. I wrote furiously as it tumbled out of her imagination. Here is one example:

THE THREE BUNNIES

By Rylie Boldt (age five)

Once upon a time there were three bunnies. They lived in a hole near somebody's house. The hole was very soft inside. The bunnies loved their home.

There was a big bunny and a middle-sized bunny. The last one was a very small bunny.

One day the three bunnies were going to eat breakfast, but it was too hot to eat. So then they hopped outside and went for a walk. And somebody forgot to close the door when they left the house.

Then a fox went into the bunnies' house. He sniffed the carrots. Then he tasted the carrots. The first carrot was too hot. The second carrot was too cold. The third carrot was just right, and he ate the whole thing.

Then the fox tried on the bunnies' boots. The first pair of boots was too big. The second pair was too small. The third pair was just right, so the fox kept them on.

Then the three bunnies came back home. They noticed there was a fox in their house. When the first bunny saw the fox, he quickly hopped back outside. When the middle-sized bunny saw the fox, she raced up to him and said, "You're never going to eat me," and ran out the door with the little bunny.

Then the biggest bunny shooed away the fox with a broom. Then the three bunnies said, "Wait a minute, Fox! Come back here with our baby's boots."

Then the three bunnies lived happily ever after. Oh, wait a minute. It's not the end of the story. Then the three bunnies got the little bunny's boots back. Then the middle-sized bunny said to the fox, "Never come back, you little skunk!"

The end.

It looks like the writing lessons at Oma's Camp are starting to take effect. Rylie's teacher wrote the following note to her mom, Michelle:

Hi Mrs. Boldt,

I just wanted to send a quick email to let you know how much I enjoy having Rylie in my class. She is so helpful, caring and kind. She is very talented in many areas that I see throughout the day but wanted to mention lately how impressed I am with her creativity in any writing assignments. I know she excels in areas where she can write, but we are just finishing up our Narratives unit and her narrative stories are fantastic! I'm very impressed! She is descriptive, engaging and hilarious in her writing. Her personality really shines through!

Just wanted to send home some "good news."

S.C.

Rylie's older brother Owen had fun writing this one:

THE PHONE CALL

By Owen Boldt (age ten)

Leanna was doing her laundry one day when the phone rang. Brrrrring! Brrrrring! Brrrrring!

"Hello," she said.

"I'm coming to your home," a cold voice said. "I'm four blocks away."

Leanna hung up the phone and kept doing laundry. Five minutes later the phone rang again. Brrrrring! Brrrrring! Brrrrring!

Leanna picked up the phone and heard the same cold voice say, "I'm three blocks away."

She hung up and dialled 911 and told the operator everything that had happened.

The operator said, "Two officers will be there in fifteen minutes."

Leanna hung up very scared. Then she heard the phone ring. Brrrrring! Brrrrring! Brrrrring! When she picked it up, she was almost too scared to answer.

"I'm on your street," the cold voice said.

Leanna was terrified. The police wouldn't be there for seven minutes. She was going to run to the garage to find a bat when the one thing she feared happened.

Knock, knock, knock!

She froze.

She slowly walked over to the door, knowing this must be the end. She reached for the doorknob and turned it. With her shaking hand, she pushed open the door. Petrified, she looked up and saw... Jimmy, the local pizza boy.

"Somebody order a pizza?" he asked.

Leanna fainted. Jimmy left the pizza on the table and walked back to his car. He wondered what that was all about.

Unexpected Guests at Oma's Writing Camp

Four grandchildren arrived on Friday for five days of learning to write and illustrate. A lot of things can happen at Oma's Camp—some of them unexpectedly. This traumatic incident at bedtime became their first writing assignment the next morning. Here is how some of them described the excitement of the first night.

CHAPTER ONE: IT ALL STARTED WITH DINNER

By Alyssa

It all started off with a perfect day. My sister Ashley and I packed all our stuff and headed off to Oma's house for some new adventures during our first ever writer's camp.

We started right away with working on our "big cheese" characters for our story. After a lot of brainstorming and stories about our own mannerisms, bad habits, and flaws, we got ready to have a delicious dinner and even more fun in the evening. Or maybe not. We had amazing spaghetti and meatballs. After dinner I went to read a book.

Suddenly, I got a pain in my stomach. At first it wasn't that bad, but it continuously got worse. A pain stabbed me like a sharp knife. It became unbearable.

I quickly told Oma what was wrong, and she said that she had a stomach ache, too. Maybe it was something we ate. The cookie dough? The meatballs? The pudding for dessert?

Little did we know my stomach ache was about to get even worse! I lay down on the couch and Oma offered me some Tums, but I couldn't take them because I kept feeling worse!

I suddenly ran to the bathroom and threw up. I felt better after that, but then I felt dizzy. I told Oma that I needed juice.

She called my parents to pick me up and I went home right away. I had some soup while watching the Phineas and Ferb show. Then I headed off to bed.

I wondered what they were doing at Oma's house while I was gone.

Probably nothing too eventful, I said to myself as I quietly dozed off. But was it?

CHAPTER TWO: EQUILIBRIUM

By Melanie

I've often thought that good and bad must be balanced. Neither one nor the other lasts forever. Oma's camp yesterday was a wonderful, awesome, marvellous experience. It stands to reason that last night was just the opposite.

I finished brushing my teeth and was about to rinse my minty toothbrush when I suddenly leapt backwards and let out a screech. Right there, not two feet away, was one of the largest bugs I've ever seen crawling out of the overflow hole in the sink. It was at least five centimetres long with countless fuzzy legs and looked drenched. In other words: terrifying, humungous, soon-to-be-squished.

The only problem was, no one was doing the squishing. Ashley walked into the washroom but didn't seem concerned about the bug. How could she be so calm? I'm deathly afraid of bugs, but I guess she isn't.

Ashley started untying her braids and told me, "Look at my pretty hair!" I laughed, but it was a breathless laugh, because I couldn't stop glancing at the monstrosity in the sink out of the corner of my eye.

We screamed for Oma to come help us, but she didn't come.

It moved! I squealed again. Ashley tried to wash it down the drain, but the bug only skittered more. I fled the washroom.

My brother Vincent yelled from behind his closed bedroom door, "Stop shouting! I'm trying to sleep!"

"There's a huge bug in the sink! You go kill it!" I yelled back, but my brother didn't answer.

Finally, Oma arrived and asked, "What's all this screaming about?"

We explained about the bug and she courageously strode into the washroom, took a piece of paper towel, and squashed the offending creature.

Whew! It was over. I could sleep now. I heaved a great sigh of relief. I rinsed my toothbrush and my mouth and got ready for bed.

Meanwhile, Ashley went back to our room.

She screamed! She ran out shouting, "There's a mouse in Alyssa's black bag!"

"A mouse?" I asked as I took a hasty step away from our doorway.

Ashley's screams brought Oma and Opa running. Ashley and I hurried upstairs. Two frights were too much! I would never be able to sleep again. I almost expected a raccoon or a skunk to jump out at me next.

I never saw the mouse, but Ashley told me it was small, black, and had beady eyes. Apparently, it ran out of our room and into Vincent's room, where Opa chased it, then killed it with Oma's shoe.

After that, Oma and Opa set all the mousetraps with peanut butter. Vincent went back to his room. Ashley and I, however, refused to sleep downstairs. Oma brought Ashley's inflatable mattress up; I decided to sleep on a couch, rather than anywhere near the sites of trauma. One incident would have been easy enough to get over, but two!

Ashley was still wide-awake and jittery. I've had pet mice before, so I wasn't as scared, but even so, those mice were in a cage.

I was exhausted, having slept only six hours the night before, but falling asleep was difficult. The washing machine hummed, the clock ticked, and the cricket chirped. The cricket was worst, because it wasn't a constant noise. It sounded as if it were in the curtains. I told myself my imagination was running wild after the previous events.

To fall asleep, I tried thinking of nothing, but of course that didn't work, so I counted until I fell into a not-so-deep slumber. The couch wasn't the most comfortable of beds, but it was a hundred times better than being downstairs, terrified that more creatures would pop out at me.

Oma's camp is exciting. I hope my theory of balance is wrong, because that would mean that more bad things are to come. What will tomorrow bring?

CHAPTER THREE: SHOCK, FEAR, AND NO SLEEP

By Ashley

It all started on a perfect camp day when one thing went wrong; there was still more to come.

I was sitting on my bed, waiting for Melanie, when I heard a scream. I had to figure out what it was, so I walked into the bathroom and saw an enormous bug with about a thousand little legs. I wasn't too scared, so I turned to look in the mirror.

Melanie looked at me and screeched, "There's a bug in the sink! Kill it."

I ignored Melanie by untying my braids. I turned to Melanie and said, "Look at my pretty hair."

"I can't believe you're messing with your hair while there's a big bug in the sink," Melanie whimpered.

"You're still worried about the bug?" I asked. I picked up a glass of water and poured it on it to wash it back down the drain, but it kept climbing up the sink.

By that time, I was scared, too.

"Oma! There's a bug in the sink!" I shouted.

After that I heard Vincent scream something about not being able to sleep. Everyone was hollering and screaming. Finally, Oma came downstairs and squished the bug and put it in the garbage.

I was walking back to our room and was about to check the black bag that Alyssa left behind when she went home sick. Suddenly, I saw a black mouse with dark eyes crawling into that bag. I freaked out and ran upstairs screaming, "Mouse! There's a mouse!" To calm down, I drank a glass of water and sat down.

Soon I saw Opa come upstairs with a squished mouse in his hand. I yelled back, "I don't want to see it!" But he showed it to me anyway. Then he threw it into the forest and washed his hands.

I decided to sleep upstairs to avoid any mice and bug attacks.

Then I went to bed, but not for long. I pushed off the covers and worried about a mouse hiding in my pillowcase or covers. I sat there with no covers, listening to Oma type on her computer. When she finished, I asked her to keep the lights on when she left.

I tried to sleep, but I heard a cricket chirping. I thought for sure it was in the bookcase beside my bed, but soon the sound seemed to have moved to another room. Also, because I had pulled off my covers, I started to freeze. I no longer cared about the mouse and put my covers back on. Then I accidentally nudged my pillow off the bed and had to get out of bed to pick it up. From all the movement, I hadn't noticed the ticking of the clock, but now I did. It lasted all night. Besides, my air mattress started deflating, so I slept with a collapsing mattress, covers bunched up around me, and my pillow over my head.

Was this all a nightmare, or was it real? That's for you to determine.

CHAPTER FOUR: WHY ME?

By Opa, the reluctant mouse chaser

The first day of Oma's Writing Camp seemed a great success. Everyone had enjoyed the activities. Now it was time for bed. Exhausted, they quietly went downstairs to prepare for a well-deserved sleep. I was only vaguely aware of what was happening, because my only involvement with Oma's camp is to oversee the kitchen. I was looking at things on my computer before heading off to bed.

Suddenly, I heard an ear-piercing scream: *"A bug, a humongous bug!"* Oh well, if it's only a bug, Oma can take care of that. She did, and all was quiet again.

Moments later, another scream loud enough to break the sound barrier. Now what? *"A mouse, there's a mouse in the black bag."* Their imagination must have gotten the better of them this time, I thought.

But this time I did go downstairs when they called for me. They pointed at the black bag that supposedly contained a mouse. Not really believing that I would find one in the bag, I picked it up and started to look through the contents. Suddenly, the cutest little mouse jumped out and scooted across the room. I tried to catch it with my bare hands without success. It ran into the hallway and then into Vincent's room.

I was still chasing it when Fern handed me her shoe and told me to kill it. Why is it that the only person in the house who objects to killing is asked to do so? What could I do? If I let the mouse escape into the storeroom, the kids would be afraid to sleep in the house.

So I did the only thing I could. One smack with the shoe was all that was needed.

After that, I had to say a quiet apology to all living things for killing one of their cutest and most innocent members. How could the poor mouse know that entering a human house is forbidden?

OMA'S CORNY JOKES

How do you stop a mouse from squeaking? Oil it.

Eighteen
The Final Oma's Camp

As the summer of 2016 approached, I wondered how Oma's Camp would work. My husband's health had deteriorated to the point where it became too stressful for him to have children romping around, making noise and needing to be fed.[10]

But I still wanted to spend time with my dear grandchildren. Since it no longer worked to have Oma's Camp at home, I had the bright idea of taking the children on a trip. But where to? How would we get there?

We finally decided to take all the available grandkids to Ottawa, the capital of Canada. My daughter-in-law Michelle volunteered to accompany us, so her young daughter Rylie could go as well. Michelle booked the hotel and arranged for our train tickets. We set the dates for August 16–19. Melanie (twenty), Vincent (sixteen), Owen (twelve), and Rylie (eight) signed up for the adventure and prepared for what would be the last Oma's Camp.[11]

Here was my note to the kids before we left:

Hi, kids! Are you getting excited about going to Ottawa with me? I sure am!
Here's a list of things to take along.
Clothes for four days
PJs
Swimsuit
Good walking shoes/socks
Toothbrush/toothpaste
Comb/brush for your hair (Yes, you must look good when you travel with your Oma!)
Your iPad, iPhone and charging cables
Your health cards

---

10 As it turned out, Peter would be diagnosed with Parkinson's disease in the fall of 2016.
11 The three oldest grandchildren, who live in California, and two others, unfortunately, couldn't make the trip.

A bit of spending money (I'll pay for your meals, but not your souvenirs)

Your train tickets

Allergy medications

A book to read on the train or before bed

Dutch Blitz to play at the hotel

Sketch pad and pencil, if you like doing that

Love, Oma

On August 16, Michelle, Owen, Rylie, and I went to the GO train station in Oakville for the first leg of the journey to Union Station in downtown Toronto, where we planned to rendezvous with Melanie and Vincent from Markham. Luckily, we all found each other.

We soon boarded the train for the four-hour ride to Ottawa. And off we went! Happy grandkids! Happy Oma, too... athough there were moments when I wondered what I had gotten myself into.

Rylie, Oma, Owen, Vincent, and Melanie on the train to Ottawa.

The kids ate many of our meals at a nearby Tim Hortons. Sniffy certainly didn't starve with all the kids' offers to share their breakfast with him.

During one meal, Michelle left the table momentarily to get something for the children. Like a naughty kid, I ripped the end of the paper covering my straw and blew through it. The paper flew several feet and landed on the floor. When Michelle returned, she reprimanded her kids for littering.

"Oma did it," they quickly admitted.

If we had brought our patience jars along, mine would have had a good measure of water dumped out.

The kids chose to visit the Royal Canadian Mint to watch the machines spit out coins. We each had a chance to lift an extremely heavy twenty-eight-pound bar of gold that was worth more than $750,000. Rylie was surprised I could lift it.[12]

Oma lifting the heavy gold bar while Rylie watches.

We visited the Parliament buildings and watched the changing of the guard. So colourful! As the drummers in the group, Owen and I loved the marching band.

When we weren't sightseeing or visiting places of interest, we played our favourite game, Dutch Blitz.

---

12 Note that it's chained to the display, so no one could run off with it.

Rylie's Lambie and my Sniffy loved all the food and amazing sites. Unfortunately, Sniffy ate way too many York peppermints and passed out on the coffee table one night in the middle of a Dutch Blitz game.

One evening, we watched the history of Canada projected onto the front of Parliament. Later, we sat on the grass and enjoyed an amazing fireworks display, the likes of which I had never seen.

No trip to Ottawa would be complete without a visit to the Byward Market. The kids each found a souvenir to take home. I found a T-shirt that said "Canadian Fast Food," with a cartoon of a bear chasing a guy. That nicked my funny bone!

Owen was in the Cadets, training to become a pilot, so he especially enjoyed our visit to the Canada Aviation and Space Museum. We had a chance to crawl into old planes and dream of flying for a few minutes.

The hotel where we stayed had a swimming pool, so I hopped in with the kids. We played Monkey in the Middle with a pair of goggles, for lack of anything else to toss from one end of the pool to the other.

Soon the four days were up, and we had to take the long train ride home. Don't ask Melanie how the sandwiches tasted that we bought. Not good!

This trip will long remain in my memory as one of the most outstanding experiences with my grandchildren.

Afterward, I wondered for a while if they would want to spend time with me and Peter anymore, now that most of them are grown up. Well, I needn't have worried. Two of them from California come for a week or more each year to stay with us. The ones who live just a few hours away visit every few weekends. The ones from St. Catharines make meals occasionally and bring them over to share with us. And yes, the visits often end up with a rousing game of Dutch Blitz. They certainly put the *grand* in grandchildren.

OMA'S CORNY JOKES

What do you call a boomerang that doesn't work? A stick.

Nineteen
A Story for Your Grandchildren

Introduction to the Mice

Hi! I'm Sniffy, and these are my two best friends, Twitch and Nibbles. Shh! I'm Oma's favourite mouse, but don't tell the other two. They might get their tails in a knot.

Twitch (four-year-old male), Sniffy (eight-year-old male), and Nibbles (six-year-old female).

I've lived at Oma's house since I was a little squeaker. My friends and I sit on her bookshelf and watch what she does. She's happiest when the grandchildren come for a visit. Every summer she invites them to come and stay for a few days of Oma's Camp. You should see them pile in the house with sleeping bags, suitcases, stuffies, backpacks, and computers. Oma smiles, leans over, and bear hugs each one as they come in. She helps them carry all their belongings to their bedrooms downstairs, but she must walk slowly, because she's getting old and out of shape.

The children can barely get to sleep the first night, because they're so excited. And Oma can't sleep with all the chattering and giggling. She reminds them two or three times that it's way past bedtime.

Would you like to know what the grandchildren do at Opa and Oma's house? If so, then snuggle up with someone you love, and I'll show you.

The Happy Face Pajamas

Sniffy, Nibbles, and Twitch gathered in a circle on a white crocheted doily on the bookshelf.

"It sounded like a crazy idea to me," Sniffy said. "But if you've met Oma, you know she does a lot of far-fetched things."

"That's for sure!" Nibbles tucked her pink tail close around her.

Twitch scooted closer to Sniffy, so he wouldn't miss any of the story. "What idea?"

"Oma decided to make a set of pyjamas for all seven of her grandchildren for Christmas," Nibbles said.

"Seven kids! Hokey doodle! That's a lot of work." Twitch slapped his cheeks with both paws. "How did she do that?"

"First, she asked all the parents to measure their kids." Sniffy showed them a tape measure that he'd taken from the sewing room.

Twitch patted his white fur. "So she would know how big their tummies were?"

"Yes, the kids are so many different sizes," Nibbles said. "She would need several patterns."

"And lots and lots of material." Twitch held his arms as far apart as he could to demonstrate.

Sniffy stroked his whiskers and continued. "Second, Oma came home with a whole bolt of flannel material with purple, red, green, and yellow happy faces on them."

"Aw! That's so cute," Twitch said.

"Third, she used the patterns to cut out nine sets of PJs," Sniffy said. "One for each grandchild, one for herself, and a baby set, in case another grandchild is born someday."

Nibbles smiled. "Smart thinking! You never know when another baby will show up."

"The fourth step was a biggie. She sewed and sewed and sewed," Sniffy said. "She complained that her fingers ached, her head hurt, and her back had a stabbing pain, but she worked late into the night for many days."

Twitch wiped a little tear from his eyes. "Aw, poor Oma."

"As she worked, she kissed some of the seams before she sewed them shut," Sniffy said.

"Why'd she do that?" Nibbles asked.

"She told Opa she was sewing love into them."

"Aw, that's so sweet," Nibbles said. "I'll bet that love never washes out either."

"And finally, when she finished," Sniffy went on, "she wrapped them up and put them away for Christmas."

Twitch started hopping up and down. "I can hardly wait to find out what happened when they opened them!"

"Look what else Oma did," Sniffy said. "She made this little book for each set of grandchildren." He reached for a copy of it from another shelf. The message on the front said *Merry Christmas, 2001, from Opa and Oma. We love you!* Below the text, she had drawn happy faces with each child's name under them.

"Let me see! Let me see!" Twitch reached for the book. "Why did she write that?"

"It explains all the special features of the pyjamas." Sniffy wiggled his backside to get comfortable and started to read. "'Number one: if you can't fall sleep, count how many happy faces are on your PJs. (That might be difficult, if the light is already out.) If that doesn't work, touch any two yellow happy faces at the same time and count to a thousand. That should do it for sure. As soon as you go to sleep, all the happy faces do, too. I hope you don't snore, or you'll wake them up and you'll have to count again.'"

"Oma snores," Twitch pointed out.

Nibbles laughed. "Does she ever! Every so often, she hits a knot when she's sawing logs. Zzzzzz, SNORK! It wakes me up."

Twitch covered his mouth with his paw and giggled.

Sniffy turned the page and kept reading. "'Number two: if you get scared during the night, there's a special "happy face button" on the front of your PJ top. Touch it and say, "Daddy loves me, Mommy loves me, Opa loves me, Oma loves me, and Jesus loves me. They won't let anyone hurt me, so I don't need to be afraid." Then you can go back to sleep.'"

Twitch reached out and touched his friend Nibbles on the shoulder. "Sometimes I'm afraid of the dark. I wish I had pyjamas with a button like that."

"That would be good," Nibbles said.

Sniffy read on. "'Number three: if you're sad, press the happy face button three times. All the faces will tickle you and make you happy again. Call Dad or Mom to show you how they do that. You probably won't need to do this often, because it's almost impossible to be sad when you're wearing PJs with so many happy faces.'" Then he reached over and tickled Twitch, who burst into more giggles.

"'I see how that works," Nibbles said. "Go on, Sniffy."

"'Number four: if you spill some jam or syrup on your PJs at breakfast, don't worry,'" he read. "'Those little guys will lick it up and their smiles will grow even larger. If they beg for more, don't give them any, or they'll eat the whole jar.'"

Nibbles checked to see if she had dribbled anything on her pink tummy at breakfast. "I'd call those self-cleaning pyjamas."

"'Number five: if your PJs get dirty," Sniffy read, "have Mom or Dad wash them in warm water and soap. Don't worry about the happy faces. They all know how to swim. Besides, you'll notice that none of them have noses. All they need to do is close their mouths and scrunch their eyes shut so they don't get soap in them. When they're clean and dry, you can wear them again. Put them on while they're still warm from the dryer.'"

Twitch wrapped his paws around himself. "I *love* to put on a shirt when it's still warm."

"The last page is about the warranty," Sniffy said.

"What's a warranty?" Nibbles asked.

"It's like a promise," Sniffy said. "'Number six: these pyjamas are guaranteed not to rip or come apart at the seams for one full year. If that happens, you get a free sleepover with Oma so she can repair them.'"

"Did the kids like their new pyjamas?" Twitch's whiskers twitched with excitement.

"Did they ever!" Sniffy said. "You should have seen how happy they were when they opened their gifts. Vincent wanted to see how the happy faces tickled him if he was sad, so his mom showed him."

"Did it work?" Twitch asked.

"It sure did!" Sniffy said. "And Oma gave one of her daughters-in-law the baby set addressed to 'Justin Case.'"

"Justin Case? Who's that?" Nibbles asked.

"Michelle didn't have any children yet, but 'just in case' she ever did, she would have a matching pair for her little one," Sniffy said.

Nibbles nodded. "Was she surprised?"

"Yes, she was. Then Oma and all the grandkids gathered on the basement steps for this photo."

"Aw!" Nibbles said. "They look so happy!"

Back: Caitlin (ten), Oma holding Vincent (one), and Amanda (eight).
Front: Melanie (five), Alyssa (five), Ashley (two), and Nicholas (six).

Conclusion

All good things must come to an end, including a week at Opa and Oma's house. This photo sums up one such week: Vincent is smiling, because he gets to stay an extra night. Owen and Rylie are sad, because it's time to return home.

Dr. Seuss said, "Don't cry because it's over; smile because it happened."[13] I'm sad that Oma's Camp is over, but I will smile the rest of my life that it happened. I love you all!

---

13 "Don't Cry Because It's Over..." *Quote Investigator*. Date of access: October 26, 2020 (https://quoteinvestigator.com/2016/07/25/smile/).